Table of Contents

Preface

The success of this book is the result of many people who have encouraged me to write. After some initial positive responses from family and friends, two groups of readers met to consider the merits of my work. The first workshop was held near Sylvan Lake and featured other chaplains and volunteers in prison ministry. I would like personally to thank the members of this group for their constructive criticism: Joan and John Palardy, Moira and Tom Brownlee, Hugo and Doreen Neufeld, Jim Shantz, Gary Garrison, Ray Landis, Elly Pauelsen, Kae Neufeld, and Peter Worsley.

The second workshop was held in conjunction with a three-month Engaging Pastors sabbatical in the fall of 2009 that I was granted by the Associated Mennonite Biblical Seminary. I met with various professors and pastors to speak about the dynamics of prison ministry. Professor Daniel Schipani offered helpful suggestions in connection with his inter-faith spiritual care workshop. Members of the reading group included Nina Lanctot, Mark Seymour, Marlin Jeschke, Joon Hyoung Park, Margaret Sawatsky, Jake Thiessen, Muriel Bechtel, Helen Lapp and others.

The academic training that I received at McGill University gave me the courage and wherewithal to undertake this project in the first place. I became convinced that a book on prison chaplaincy is necessary to help newer chaplains gain appreciation of the wide-ranging nature of prison ministry. I was fairly naïve when I began ministry. I soon learned that there are many challenges for which one needs to be prepared theologically, emotionally, socially, and clinically. I trust that the glimpses I offer in this book will be a window into these opportunities.

In conclusion, I would like to thank the mentors who have been key to my chaplaincy journey. I think first and foremost of Reverend Tilman Martin, who in his quiet manner showed me the things that I should and should not do. More recently, Joan Palardy, a Catholic colleague, has been indispensible in showing me what prison chaplaincy is all about. I am not sure I would have remained in chaplaincy were it not for her vision and empathy.

There are, of course, a myriad of saints that could be mentioned. Ronald George Labonté became a dear friend and colleague in Quebec, Gabriel Savignac helped me trim my rougher edges, and Pierre Allard showed all of us the way forward. Then there are John and Ruth Hess, Evelyn Mackenzie, Carol Murdoch, Tom Harrison, and many others. For them all, I am truly grateful.

Foreword

It is an honour to write a foreword for this lovely set of reflections on a lifetime of fine pastoral ministry. The ministry of this author is wonderfully normal, even exceptionally so, but the setting is unfamiliar for many in the faith communities. It is this unique setting that gives bold relief to the historic value of quality pastoral care and of the ministry of Don Stoesz.

Personally, I had never expected to serve in the correctional world, even though early on I received encouragement from a wise old priest. His wisdom proved prophetic, and 15 years or so after ordination there I was. After almost ten happy years in the trenches of the Montreal Prison at Bordeaux, I spent fifteen years with some fine and visionary people in providing leadership for the Chaplaincy program of the Correctional Service of Canada. In this interval, chaplaincy interventions expanded greatly – and came to include not just the prisoner, but also the volunteers with their many gifts and deep commitment to safe communities, the community systems which helped integrate the released prisoner, the family of the prisoner who served the sentence in their own way, the victims, and, through all that, the staff. The context for this ministry evolved as well. From hiring an individual to do chaplaincy, the process became more complicated but with enormous possibilities for further development by hiring the chaplain through a contract with a faith community. This provided an improved opportunity for partnership between the Correctional Service of Canada and the civilian faith community. The context spread beyond the boundaries of Canada and the shores of North America. We entered into dialogue and sharing with other chaplaincy services the world over. My original expectations were quite simply, and thankfully, wrong.

During this period, the chaplaincy department, increasingly confident of its capacity to contribute, became part of the "correctional team." Meetings within the chaplaincy department alone were rare – other departments joined us, or we them, depending on the issue. A lone wolf approach became not only impossible, but desperately weak. Careful research, active imagination, serious thought and a commitment to service gave rise to some unique interventions. One of special note was the development of the *Circle of Support and Accountability (CoSA)*. This community-based model evolved to assist the safe reintegration of the most feared sexual offenders into the community. Research showed it to be a very worthwhile model. It was picked up around the world.

It was in this growing and evolving ministry that I came to know and enjoy Don Stoesz. Don Stoesz has had an enormous background of thoughtful ministry in the world of corrections (perhaps surprisingly so, as it was for me). While a prison chaplain, he faithfully attended theological conferences where he presented different papers on his unique ministry experience.

His interests are wide ranging, "catholic" in the root meaning of that word. They frequently embrace apparent opposites. He has a rich academic and literary background and he works in a culture where illiteracy is a huge problem. He is endued with a wonderful sense of ecumenism, of the wonders of the wider Christian and religious spectrum, and he knows the crucial importance of faithful loyalty to one's God within a smaller denomination. He thinks about the practical details of daily ministry and he wrestles with the bigger conceptual ideas of justice, ecclesiology and theology. He thinks energetically about the highlights and writes compassionately about the times ministry can go sideways. He is fluent in the two founding Canadian cultures, French and English, and speaks with respect, sympathy, vigour, and sometimes humour, of many other cultures that often clash in the correctional boiling pot.

This challenging and wonderful book will be of interest to many people.

- The most obvious group of readers will be those interested in prison ministry: volunteers, committed staff, new and veteran chaplains. They will all find this an important and unique resource.
- Many other persons impacted by our criminal justice system, prisoners, staff, families of offenders, victims, will find these reflections of interest. It will feed their yearning to live helpfully.
- Persons who are looking for fresh takes on the big theological and pastoral issues of our day, wherever they live or work, will find stimulation and food for thought in this work. The setting is unique; the issues are universal.
- And last but not least, persons looking for spiritual enrichment could place this book by their bedside table and read a page before going to sleep. The format of one page reflections and an appropriate scripture quotation make it a rich devotional book. The test of all good theology is its helpfulness in the spiritual journey.

Rev. Canon Chris Carr
Retired Director General, Chaplaincy Department
Correctional Service of Canada
Wolfe Island, ON.
May 2010

Glimpses of Grace:

Reflections of a Prison Chaplain

Introduction

Anyone who has seen the musical, *Les Miserables,* remembers the act of grace that Bishop Bienvenu (Welcome) bestows on the convict Jean Valjean. The bishop invites Jean Valjean for supper and lets him stay the night in his small manse. Jean Valjean returns the favour by stealing the plates and silverware from the bishop's bedroom and fleeing into the night.

The police catch up with Jean Valjean the next day. They discover the valuable objects in his bag and escort him back to the bishop's residence. They ask the bishop whether the man stole the treasured objects. Bishop Bienvenu responds by saying that he gave Jean the plates and silverware. He goes further by producing two silver candlesticks and giving them to Jean Valjean. "Here," the bishop retorts, "You forgot to take these along with your plates. They should fetch about two hundred francs."[1]

Thus begins a long story of redemption for Jean Valjean. He has no idea how to live in society. He has served nineteen years behind bars for stealing a loaf of bread. He has escaped numerous times, been recaptured, and been given more time for his attempts at freedom. All he can think of while lying awake in the middle of the night in the bishop's house is the value of the plates off which he ate that evening. He thinks only of himself and what he can get out of the situation. He even contemplates murdering the holy man before absconding with the merchandise.

The bishop's act of kindness and generosity gives Jean a second chance. Jean Valjean goes on to become a respected businessman in a small French town. He is elected to the position of mayor after several years of declining the invitation. He is the chief employer of a "jet-work" factory that produces jewellery and ornaments. He becomes known as Father Madeleine as well as Monsieur the Mayor.[2] The bishop's epitaph appears to have come true: "You belong no longer to evil, but to good. It is your soul that I am buying for you. I withdraw it from dark thoughts and from the spirit of perdition, and I give it to God."[3]

Most people fail to remember that Jean Valjean goes on to steal again on the very same day that the bishop gave him his new equity on life. As he leaves the bishop's village, Jean encounters a young Savoyard who is tossing some coins in the air. Jean places his heavy foot over a forty-sou piece that has fallen to the ground. When Petit Gervais asks for it back, Jean shoos him away with these words, "You'd better take care of yourself."[4] The boy flees in terror.

Jean immediately regrets what he has done. He searches in vain for the boy to give the money back. He encounters a priest and gives him some money "for the poor." He tells the priest, "Monsieur Abbe, have me arrested. I am a robber." The priest flees.[5]

This seemingly insignificant act follows Jean for the rest of the book. Javert, a police constable, meets Jean Valjean as Monsieur Mayor on a chance encounter. He recognizes Jean as the old convict and links him to the theft of the money from Petit Gervais.[6] He pursues every angle to have Jean Valjean arrested and tried. He is ultimately successful, but stops at the final moment when he realizes that Jean has saved him from death at the hands of French revolutionaries. Unable to live with the paradox between retributive justice and merciful response, he commits suicide. Jean Valjean is finally free to reveal his identity. He can now live with acceptance and peace as part of his newly adopted family.

Justification, Sanctification, and Judgment

This story mirrors the journey I take with many offenders. Like Jean Valjean, the first act of mercy and forgiveness that offenders experience overwhelms them. They realize the extent to which they have harmed others. They begin to understand the amount of anger and rage they have carried for so many years. They see that there is a way out of their deeply entrenched patterns of behaviour. Victor Hugo recounts Jean Valjean's remorse in this way:[7]

"He felt dimly that the pardon of this priest was the hardest assault, and the most formidable attack which he had yet sustained; that his hardness of heart would be complete, if he resisted this kindness; that if he yielded, he must renounce that hatred with which the acts of other men had for so many years filled his soul, and in which he found satisfaction; that, this time, he must conquer or be conquered, and that the struggle, a gigantic and decisive struggle, had begun between his own wickedness, and the goodness of this man."

I have the privilege of walking alongside many men who have experienced this moment of justification for the first time. They have poured out their hearts as they have recounted the variety of circumstances and situations that have caused them to come to jail. Many of them have told me that they would now be dead if they had not been arrested. Others have told me that they never imagined that things would get this bad. "I am not a violent person," they tell me. Some of them are doing life sentences while still others will never be released from prison. The moment of justification is so real because of the many years of hard living that have made them into bitter and vengeful human beings. They could just as easily kill the person beside them as weep with anguish for the suffering they have caused and experienced.

The Jean Valjean story is powerful because the experience of justification happens at the beginning of the book. This is different from the conversion stories with which I grew up. The teenage adventures that were featured in the Danny Orlis series of the 1950s ended with a conversion experience on page ninety-eight of a one-hundred-and-thirteen page book. The implicit message within these Bernard Palmer stories is that a Nicodemus-like rebirth is the most important aspect of the Christian faith. Conversion is the climax of the story rather than its beginning.

A similar trend is evident in the jail-house conversion stories featured in the Chaplain Ray series. These books have been so successful because of the dramatic change that is evident in ex-offenders. The former lives of these born-again Christian men have been so horrible that their change is a miracle to behold. Their testimonies speak volumes about the possibility of transformation that Jesus Christ has to offer.

The dramatic nature of these stories sometimes overshadows the real work of transformation that is going on in the lives of believers. We as Christians are drawn to the sensational. We tend to overlook the more mundane aspects of support and accountability that is needed to keep us on the "straight and narrow."

This is why the story of Jean Valjean is so compelling. Victor Hugo knows that it will take another twenty years of Jean's life to make a complete turnaround. Jean has to learn how to love, how to care, how to be honest, and how to return good for evil. These aspects of Jean's transformation are featured in the rest of the eleven hundred pages of Hugo's *magnum opus.*

Victor Hugo is well aware of the stigma of incarceration that ex-offenders carry with them. The dire effect of this disgrace is poignantly illustrated near the end of the book when Jean reveals who he is to his new son-in-law. Marius has the following thoughts on the matter:[8]

"He (Jean) was a convict; that is, the creature, who, on the social ladder, has no place, being below the lowest round. After the lowest of men, comes the convict. The convict is no longer, so to speak, the fellow of the living. The law has deprived him of all humanity which it can take from a man. . . . He (Marius) thought it natural that certain infractions of the written law should be followed by eternal penalties, and he accepted social damnation as growing out of civilization."

This harsh judgment is all too real for the men with whom I work. Most of society feels their job is done when the criminal has been caught, tried, convicted, and sentenced. The climax of the story occurs on the six o'clock news when the murderer is sentenced to life imprisonment. Few people are interested in what occurs in the next twenty-five years of the person's life.

Sentencing is similar to justification in that it creates a euphoric feeling that justice has been served. The inmate is convicted in both senses of the word. In the case of the courts, he or she has been found guilty by the law and sentenced accordingly. In the case of faith, he or she has been convicted by the Holy Spirit and comes to repentance. Unfortunately, the latter experience often occurs after the former. Justification of faith takes place within a context where a person still has to pay for his or her sins in the real terms of a prison sentence.

It is within this triangle of judgment, justification, and sanctification that real change can take place. I have written this book to help others see that emphasizing any one of these themes to the exclusion of the other can have dire results. To err on the side of judgment is to turn deserved consequences into vindictive punishment. To err on the side of justification is to place unrealistic expectations on the spiritual euphoria of release. To err on the side of sanctification is to forgive others less than seventy times seven for their humanity. Each of these themes has to be viewed in the context of the other in order to be viable.

Cathartic Effects of Prison Life

Any new staff person or volunteer who walks into a prison finds out how intense an atmosphere prison life can be. Inmates share their fears about being attacked by other inmates. They talk about their feelings of claustrophobia for being locked up for long stretches of time. They speak about the shame, guilt, and humiliation they experience as a result of the crimes they have committed. Inmates come to prison with many of the same behaviours they exhibited on the street. Some are addicts and get heavily in debt by continuing to use drugs in prison. Some are naïve and are taken advantage of by their peers.

Bullying and settling conflicts by violence is viewed as normal in a prison context. Offenders live by an "inmate code" where informants are severely punished for "ratting" on their fellow residents. A pecking order of crimes is established which places murderers and drug dealers on top of the heap while pedophiles and rapists are seen as the "lowest of the low." Inmates who try to break out of this code are at risk of retribution.

The prison atmosphere has a cauldron effect in which the heat of these pressures makes inmates take a serious look at themselves and their actions. They find out who they can live with, who they can trust, how to mind one's own business, and how to solve problems in the five minutes of prison justice that is allotted to their case. Behaviours from which a person can run away on the street are all too visible in the fishbowl of a living unit. Inmates have to learn to take responsibility for their actions as well as be willing to challenge others who are taking advantage of them. This learning curve is too much for some.

One of the curious results of this crucible of care is that it can either make an inmate better or worse. Inmates come to see me because they realize for the first time how much change has to happen if they are ever going to live in society again. They are willing to work the twelve steps of Alcoholics Anonymous. They share deeply about their lives and crimes. They devour any literature on faith and grace that they can get their hands on. They search out volunteers who are willing to listen to them. They appreciate the music and worship ministry. They admit that they have a long way to go. They are openly vulnerable in their frank acknowledgement of deeply seated sin.

This is, perhaps, as it should be. Anyone who has been convicted of a serious crime has had to face facts which up to now have remained hidden. No one knew that the friendly restaurant owner sold drugs. No one knew that there was a marriage problem in the family. No one knew who had killed their friend in a late-night brawl. Inmates have learned to live a double life-style for so long that it comes as a shock as well as a relief when it is finally over. Their lives, as Alcoholics Anonymous puts it, have become unmanageable. Inmates are searching for a whole new way of life to replace the one they have lived up to now.

The cauldron of recriminations, contracts, suspicion, accusations, and bitterness of prison life can also have the opposite effect. Several inmates who saw some hope when I first met them turned over time into such men of stone that I no longer knew how to reach them. Forgiveness, grace, love, and a conscience no longer appeared to be real. These offenders became better criminals and worse murderers rather than better men. I do not know what the breaking point was in their lives. Many of these men are now either dead or doing life sentences in prison. Prison can make a person worse as well as better.

Role of a Chaplain

One of the first obligations of a prison chaplain is to accommodate different religious practices. Each inmate has a right by law to practice his or her faith within a prison setting. The task of a chaplain is to ascertain the nature of that religion, verify the special food diets and festivals associated with that faith, and provide space and time for these religious events to take place.

The second task of a chaplain is to work ecumenically with his or her chaplaincy colleagues. Catholic and Protestant chaplains have historically been assigned to each prison setting. More recently, Jewish, Islamic, Wiccan, and Sikh chaplains have been hired to reflect the religious diversity of inmate populations. While there used to be separate Catholic and Protestant chapels, many institutions now have one multi-faith sanctuary to accommodate diverse religious rituals. Flexibility and mutual respect are key ingredients in making chaplaincy effective within this environment.

A third task of a chaplain is to provide religious services reflective of his or her faith tradition. I and a Protestant colleague facilitate a worship service that mirrors the liturgical tradition of the mainline churches. While I am Mennonite and he is Missionary Alliance, we have found that a liturgical service with the various prayers of confession, prayers of the faithful, scripture readings, homily, singing, and communion has provided the most continuity within what can be quite a chaotic atmosphere. This "ordered" service has the added benefit of dovetailing closely with the Catholic Mass. Offenders learn to affirm the commonality within different Christian denominations.

We as chaplains consider the congregation that gathers on Sunday evenings within prison to be part of the larger body of Christ. Although we do not encourage baptism, confessions of faith are offered and communion is celebrated within a body of believers who confess Jesus Christ as their Saviour and Lord. Offenders serve as presiders, are part of the worship band, read scriptures, help serve communion, and offer prayers for each other and the larger community. Volunteers make up part of this congregation through their weekly attendance and participation.

The sense of community that is created comes with the same set of problems that congregations experience in society. Musically-minded offenders disagree over who should be in the band. Some question the authenticity of their fellow Christians' testimonies. Others have little understanding of faith, much less communion. Still others are not willing to give a handshake of peace to their peers. These problems are intrinsic to any faith group that is attempting to become a collective body.

A fourth task of a chaplain involves providing pastoral care to his or her parishioners. A chaplain learns to move beyond the superficial spiritual talk that can result from men who are looking for acceptance and belonging within a prison environment. Offenders learn that it is safe to speak about the deeply seated reasons that have brought them to prison. They slowly allow the vulnerability of their emotional and social lives to be integrated into their newly-found faith. Maturity and insight are the result of this holistic approach.

A fifth challenge of a chaplain is providing programs that represent a bridge between the pastoral focus of chaplaincy and the psychologically-oriented programming of the institution. Alternatives to Violence, Christopher Leadership, and Grief Recovery courses encourage inmates to become pro-social while learning leadership and conflict resolution skills in the process. Group sharing helps offenders break down their inhibitions and fears. Offenders find that these programs offer them a way out of the anti-social tendencies that have become habits.

A pastoral presence to staff is another opportunity that a chaplain has to offer. Many staff are bound to specific tasks and objectives within their own departments. A chaplain is free to visit all parts of the prison and communicate with all levels of administration. The open-ended nature of a chaplain's job enables him or her to boost morale, defuse potential conflict situations, and step into situations that would otherwise require more heavy-handed approaches. A chaplain has the rare opportunity to build social bonds that may be lacking within and between departments. Positive morale can easily be lost in a place that is preoccupied with security. General goodwill can slip into suspicion and accusation if not caught in time.

Journey to Sanctification

We need to return to the story of Jean Valjean to consider the factors that changed his life. His journey of healing and hope will help us understand how we can be restored to wholeness and integrity.

Half-way through the book, Jean Valjean goes into hiding from Javert and the other French police. He scales the wall of a convent and becomes a fellow gardener with an old acquaintance. He has with him a young girl by the name of Cosette. She is the daughter of a woman named Fantine who died while in the employ of Jean Valjean, then known as Monsieur Madeleine. Jean feels responsible for Fantine's death and vows to raise Cosette as his own. She is accepted into the convent as a novitiate.

Jean's maturation from justification to sanctification occurs during this time. He observes the nuns in their acts of voluntary penance and self-sacrifice. He compares this self-imposed spiritual slavery to the involuntary punishment he endured for so many years in prison:[9]

"And in these two places, so alike and yet so different, these two species of human beings so dissimilar were performing the same work of expiation. . . Jean Valjean thoroughly comprehended the expiation of the first; personal expiation, expiation for oneself. But he did not understand that of the others, of these blameless spotless creatures, and he asked himself with a tremor: "Expiation of what? What expiation?" . . A voice responded in his conscience; the most divine of all human generosity, expiation for others."

Jean Valjean is transported from the release of justification to a commitment of care that he experiences in this convent. He realizes that it is possible to "gain the whole world" by denying oneself. The remaining attributes of pride, defiance, and hard heartedness are dispelled as Jean offers daily prayers of penance outside the window of the chapel where the nuns are lying prostrate before the altar of God. "His whole heart melted in gratitude, and he loved more and more."[10]

Saint Paul has something to say about this transformation of grace. He suggests that it is better to love than to have all the hope and faith in the world. Hope and Faith are precious commodities in prison. There are some inmates who waste away after many years of incarceration because they have given up hope. The light at the end of the tunnel has been extinguished. They hope only for death, self-inflicted or otherwise. Others cling to knowledge of the Bible as though that is their saving grace. They tell me what scripture texts mean in the original Hebrew and Greek and encourage me to improve my meditations. They wonder about the orthodoxy of my faith and are not shy in helping to correct me.

Paul's advice to love is a formidable one that has to be seen in the context of these other virtues. A chaplain discovers that he or she cannot link his or her care to the inmate's success. I have seen the same persons come back to jail time and time again over the ten years that I have known them. I realize that Paul's advice was not given lightly. We cannot have only hope for that person or link his faith to the possibility of success. We have to learn to love in a way that is free of human expectations. I can only continue in prison ministry if I take Paul's advice in I Corinthians 13 seriously.

The mutual transformation of chaplain and offender ensures the future of care within a prison context. Chaplains can not last in prison ministry if they have not allowed themselves to be transformed by the acts of grace that are offered. Last week, an offender helped me understand the difference between Pentecostal and Ukrainian Catholic forms of worship. "Pentecostals are not shy to intrude on the presence of God," he stated. "They really rock. Catholics are much more afraid (respectful) of what that means." What an insight into how differently true devotion is interpreted. Just yesterday, an inmate returned some things he had taken from my office. He told me, "I bet you don't get a lot of offenders returning things that they have stolen from you." I had to agree. He then said, as a way of incriminating himself, "I bet you don't get a lot of guys stealing things from your office." I had to agree a second time.

Format of the Book

Pastoral care within prison occurs within a transient setting in which a one-hour conversation of deep emotion and faith is sometimes the only contact the chaplain has with an offender. Constant demands within an ever changing environment mean that a chaplain has to take the time to digest each precious moment of grace that comes along. There is an almost complete turn-over of the prison population every five years. A chaplain has to learn what he or she can give in each context.

This book has been structured with some of this "frenetic" energy in mind. One hundred and twenty-one glimpses of grace have been capsulated within one-page vignettes. Most vignettes include a description of an encounter, a reflection on that experience, and a scripture verse at the bottom that may be pertinent. Some reflections are more didactic in the sense that they comment more broadly on the dynamics of prison ministry. Movies, books, and theoretical themes provide the backdrop of these latter vignettes.

The mutual transformation of chaplain and offender is illustrated in these pastoral moments. Some interviews come to an abrupt halt when the chaplain or offender realizes that the conversation has gone beyond what he or she expected. Other discussions reveal that the offender has much more resentment and anger toward his sentence than he realized. Some offenders expect the chaplain to have all the answers. They sit quietly in the office waiting for the chaplain to steer the conversation.

These encounters have given me much to think about. In what situations am I effective as a chaplain? In what areas do I need to improve? I have grown spiritually as I have become involved in the lives of prisoners and the life of the institution.

The book has been divided into two parts and eleven chapters to reflect the diverse nature of chaplaincy. The first part of the book deals with direct ministry opportunities. The second half reflects more broadly on the theoretical and theological implications of chaplaincy.

Spiritual care has been selected as the first chapter because this is the hub around which many other activities and relationships revolve. A chaplain's ability to identify with the suffering, anxiety, assurance, and faith of an offender is what fuels his or her chaplaincy. Programs, administrative work, diverse religious expressions, and meaningful worship services flow from the centrality of care that is exhibited by a chaplain.

Involvement in family relationships follows as a natural consequence of becoming acquainted with an offender. Inmates are preoccupied with the loss of relationships that have resulted from their offences. Chaplains help inmates deal with the grief, broken trust, and loneliness they experience while incarcerated. Inmates slowly allow themselves to replace wishful thinking about the past with hopeful signs within the present.

Issues of authority are paramount in a chaplain's work because of its central role within an institution. Offenders are in prison because they have either taken the law into their own hands or been in defiance of it. They are under the external authority of prison staff because they have never learned to internalize limits for themselves. Inmates have to learn to become adults all over again within the context of a repressive environment. This is not an easy thing to do for many inmates.

Therapeutic models of ministry are needed to help a chaplain deal with the many dysfunctional behaviours and attitudes that he or she observes. Each chaplain learns to depend on a few resources that are effective in addressing these issues. Harville Hendrix's book on marriage, <u>Getting the Love You Want</u>,[11] is invaluable in understanding relationships. Bruno Bettleheim's book on fairy tales, <u>Uses of Enchantment</u>,[12] has helped offenders move from paralysis to empowerment and engagement. Each chaplain is drawn to a different set of books and skills that help him or her in the clinical aspects of prison ministry. See the Bibliography for the books referred to in these pages.

Group sessions provide an excellent means of demonstrating the difference between what is said in a chaplain's office and how inmates respond in a social setting. In spite of the best intentions, all of us find it hard to practice what we preach. Programs such as Grief Recovery, Christopher Leadership, and Alternatives to Violence provide social venues by which offenders learn to interact with others. These courses echo the social dynamics that are found in congregations. Bible studies, music ministry, and congregational involvement are ways of helping offenders learn what being part of a body is all about.

Volunteers are a natural extension of a chaplain's ministry. They are the citizens of the community who come face to face with the inmates who have offended against people in society. These encounters make for a dynamic relationship in which volunteers learn how they can contribute to an offender's success. Volunteers' testimonies inspire offenders and give them hope. Jailhouse habits and lingo become diffused within social settings that involve outside guests.

Part II of this book reflects more broadly on the ecumenical, multi-faith, and theological implications of prison ministry. A theoretical model is needed to address this richness of experience. I cite specific incidents and examples to illustrate the ways in which I have been "stretched" in these encounters.

Ecumenism obviates the competitive spirit that is sometimes evident in the evangelistic efforts of various denominations. Christians within prison learn to work together with others in order to reflect a commonality of spirit. Much is left by the wayside as Christians learn to focus on what is essential to faith.

A similar dynamic is at work in relation to other religions. Chaplains, volunteers, and offenders find out that "putting down" another religion is a very weak means of promoting one's own faith. Learning to articulate the redemptive experiences within our own lives goes a long way to making others feel at home in our worship services.

Restorative Justice, outlined in the ninth chapter, is a theme that is integral to prison ministry. The twelve steps of Alcoholics Anonymous speak explicitly about becoming reconciled to God, oneself, and one's victims. All three are needed for healing and hope to take place. Becoming reconciled to oneself and God is the most immediate way that chaplains are involved with offenders in their journey. Becoming restored in relationship to victims and their families is an infinitely more complicated process. In some cases, Restorative Justice feels like an ever-receding horizon. Forgiveness may not be humanly possible. There is too much justifiable anger on the part of the victims. Many offenders work hard at bringing healing in whatever way they can.

The ecclesiastical implications of chaplaincy is the tenth theme of this book. One of the curious results of working as a minister within a penal setting is that the two "institutional" contexts of church and prison are sometimes at odds. While God forgives a person, the justice system asks for demonstration of remorse. While God restores a person to his or her divinely created nature, the Correctional Service remains sceptical of a person's possibilities of transformation. While I as a pastor assert that believers within prison are part of the universal body of Christ, the prison system separates this body by a fence line. The fact that the church represents a "parallel" body of correction and restoration makes for interesting discussions in my work with the Correctional Service of Canada.

There are many theological implications that follow from these pastoral reflections. Sin is more deeply rooted than first imagined. The will of God is more powerful than human will. True transformation takes a long time. Prison ministry offers us an opportunity to get along with others who are very different. Can you imagine living next door to a pedophile, downstairs from a murderer, and one living unit away from the person who testified against you in your trial? Can you imagine having Sikhs, Muslims, Jehovah's Witnesses, atheists and Wiccans in addition to Christians as part of your worship service? Can you imagine having severe addiction issues where a pouch of tobacco costs $500 and you earn $5 a day? Who are you going to phone to help pay your debts? All of these realities shape the way that offenders, prison staff, and chaplains think about what it means for God to be present. Theological reflections on these themes represent the final chapter of the book.

Some Final Points of Clarification

Some final points of clarification are in order. I serve under contract with my denomination, the Mennonite Church, to provide chaplaincy services within the Correctional Service of Canada. The chaplaincy department of CSC is responsible for hiring me as well as providing monies to my denomination for my salary. My denomination is responsible for credentialing me as well as overseeing my ministry.

I am writing this book as a Christian chaplain with a view to dialogue with a broader audience. My Christian faith has been enhanced and deepened as I have rubbed shoulders with believers of many different religions and different walks of life. I have been challenged to think about why I am a Christian, why I am a member of a church, and why I consider the Bible to be sacred.

The opportunity for discussion with a broader faith community is illustrated by the cover of this book. Early on in my ministry, an offender gave me a chalk drawing of a sunflower with a horizon backdrop of sun and moon. It resonates with what I know about the life and work of Vincent Van Gogh. The sunflower was Van Gogh's favourite flower. "Yellow" was his favourite colour. The red and white lines around the moon and sun were van Gogh's way of symbolizing the mystical aspects of life. This drawing is similar to van Gogh's *Starry Night.*[13]

Van Gogh was asked why he did not paint images of Jesus like his contemporaries, Bernard and Gauguin. Van Gogh replied that it was not necessary to "offer tenderness and consolation" by presenting "the main character of the Sermon on the Mount."[14] He would rather paint natural scenes of olive trees than the Garden of Gethsemane itself (*Olive Trees with Yellow Sky and Sun).*[15] The suffering that Jesus underwent in this garden is evoked in van Gogh's painting of a harsh sun, barren ground, shadows, and the menacing appearance of leaf clusters. These natural images *stand in* for the religious symbolism of the suffering of Christ.

A similar dynamic is at work on the front cover of this book. It represents hope of a better life for the inmate who gave it to me. It offers signs of redemption as we wake up to face the sun by day and moon by night. There is opportunity for blossoming together with the sunflower in its ripeness. There is thankfulness for the nourishment that we receive at the gracious hands of faith. The themes of justification, love, sanctification, and hope that are offered to me through Christ are extended "as if" by osmosis through this painting to people of other faiths.

Another point I need to clarify is that I have worked primarily with male offenders within the federal prison system of Canada. The stories that are included in this book are reflective of the work that I have done with these men.

Women offenders are housed in separate facilities and have access to chaplains who work in those institutions.

Men who have been sentenced to more than two years of incarceration serve time within a federal prison. Provincial jails house offenders who are serving sentences for less than two years. Men who have been convicted of first degree murder serve a minimum of twenty-five years in prison before they are eligible for parole. They are serving a life sentence in the sense that they are accountable to the Correctional Service of Canada for the rest of their lives.

I have tried to keep the identities of staff and inmates illustrated in this book as confidential and anonymous as possible. Many stories represent a collage of different personalities and experiences. The names have been changed.

In conclusion, I trust that the short vignettes in this book will give the reader a better understanding of the dynamics of prison ministry. May the window provided by these brief glimpses allow the light of the gospel to shine into the corners of life.

Donald Stoesz
Lent, 2010

– PART I –

- Chapter One -

Opportunities for Spiritual Transformation

1. Innocence and Guilt

It is impossible to count the number of times that an offender has informed me that he is innocent of the crime of which he has been convicted. Most of the crimes are quite serious. Offenders receive sentences of between three years and life for what they have done. These claims of innocence have led me to the polarized conclusion that either a great travesty of justice has occurred or human beings are capable of minimizing the reality of a situation to a much greater extent than I thought possible.

One particular example comes to mind. Henry had been fighting for his innocence during the past fifteen years. He was hoping the Supreme Court of Canada would look into his case. One day, he stated his line of reasoning to me: "They only found blood on the outside, not the inside of the car. How could they have convicted me?" My instant thought was: "What was blood doing on the outside of the car?"

Henry carved exquisite miniature wooden wagons that he made in the hobby shop and sold to various staff members. He came to me because one of these wagons had been extensively damaged in transit from another penitentiary. Henry's suspicion was that the damage had been done deliberately and with *evil* intent. As I went through the channels of bureaucracy to find out what had happened, I marvelled at the incongruity of the situation. Here was a man who had been convicted of a heinous murder and yet was able to work gently with the most delicate of hobby crafts. Perhaps God was paying him recompense. Maybe this man was trying to show the world how gentle and caring he was, in spite of the crime of which he had been convicted. Although I will never know whether or not Henry was innocent, he did teach me a valuable lesson that day. May we all be so inclined in our gentle touch.

Look at the birds of the air; they neither sow nor reap nor gather into barns, and yet your heavenly Father feeds them. Are you not of more value than they? (Matthew 6:26)

2. *Never Judge a Book by its Cover*

One of the difficult challenges of prison ministry is to discern whether offenders are telling the truth. Some inmates are so used to making things up as they go along that they think nothing of leading staff and chaplains and volunteers astray. A good illustration of this challenge came in the form of an interview to hire a chapel cleaner. One of the candidates clearly stood out for his neat appearance, work experience, polite manner, and communication skills. Ralph came highly recommended by his parole officer.

Ralph proved to be a hard worker who kept the chapel clean, got along with his co-workers, and shared personal information about his life. He successfully completed a "Reasoning and Rehabilitation" program during this time. We came to rely on Ralph because of his personable manner and easygoing personality.

One Monday morning we were cleaning up after a Family Worship Service. Ralph mentioned that he had noticed Conrad go into the women's bathroom with his wife Julia. This information was a little startling. Although this type of behaviour was known to happen, Conrad had always been respectful in the past. I felt that I needed to confront Conrad as a result of this information. I met with him in my office. Conrad was so upset at this allegation that he left my office and came back later to say that nothing of the sort had happened. I should check my source of information.

With a growing knot in my stomach, and a sixth sense question from another chaplain, I delved deeper into Ralph's past record. I discovered that he had been transferred from another institution because of a false accusation he had made against someone there. It was Ralph who was the problem -- not Conrad and Julia.

We never found out why Ralph felt it necessary to make this allegation against one of his co-inmates. Why would Ralph point a finger at a respected individual, knowing that this type of behaviour had gotten him into trouble in the past? That question remains unanswered.

A humorous side to this story came a few weeks later when Ralph returned to the chapel to show us a picture of his fancy red sports car. It was true that we could recognize him in the picture. As far as we were concerned, however, Ralph could have had that picture taken in front of a sports car that belonged to someone else.

For all who do evil hate the light and do not come to the light, so that their deeds may not be exposed (John 3:20).

3. When the Other Shoe Drops

Chaplains receive requests for emergency phone calls, religious diets, counselling sessions, Bible study courses, baptismal procedures, faith issues, and conflict resolution. The initial requests often appear superficial. The person is wondering when chapel services are scheduled, what church groups are providing ministry, and what Bible studies are available. Personal issues usually have to do with adjustments to the institution, visitation of family members, or a crisis in relation to getting along with a roommate.

The chaplain soon learns that these initial encounters have little to do with the real reason the person has sought help. These initial forays are simply a testing ground to see how open the chaplain is to working with some unspoken requests. Sometimes, these hidden agendas are intended for ill. This is known as an "anatomy of a set-up." Perhaps the offender wants to ask a favour that would not be possible to grant through other means.

Often the offender is seeking to deal with issues for which he has few means to handle. Many offenders are too proud or too suspicious or too afraid to ask for help. In over sixty percent of the cases, the damage has already been done. All I can do is help the offender grieve over the many losses of family, children, and friends that have and will continue to occur.

The chaplain has an opportunity to get to know the person so that some of these issues can be spoken about before he experiences more grief. The offender often wishes to discuss things that are of such a serious nature that he does not know where to begin. He knows that by identifying areas in his life that need work, he is opening himself to correction as well as admitting to himself and others that he needs to change. This is when the "other shoe" drops. He and the chaplain began with some fairly basic discussions of faith and love. The conversation suddenly veers into deeper water for which neither person is prepared. A decision has to be made to either keep going or abruptly suspend the dialogue. Both alternatives are well travelled routes that require discernment.

Always be ready to make your defence to anyone who demands from you an accounting for the hope that is in you (1 Peter 3:15).

4. The Guys Who Get Worse

One of the sad realities of prison ministry is that there are some men with whom I have worked who have gotten worse. I am thinking particularly of three men I got to know over a two-year period. Each was serving between two and four years for assaults and a home invasion. Each was involved in chapel services and came for about ten to fifteen counselling sessions.

Each of these men had some serious problems for which they were seeking help. I was able to help at least one of them while the other two continued to experience serious relationship, anger, and emotional problems. The men felt safe enough to speak about their identity issues, emotional upheavals, and in two cases, dysfunctional family dynamics.

Each of these men was released into the community after serving their sentence. They each were convicted of first degree murder within two years of returning to society. This is a sobering reality. I knew that these men were mixed up. The Correctional Service knew some of the risk factors in each of their cases. Nothing prepared me for the news that these men were now serving a life sentence with no chance for parole for twenty-five years. These men will be about sixty years old before they have a chance to be released into the community again. Given their history, this opportunity may never be granted.

What is it about human nature that leads to such evil acts? Why did these men act so violently again? They had already tasted the negative consequences of prison life. I do not know the answer to these questions. I am reluctant to get in touch with the men to ask them. The pastoral friendship that we had is too painful to remember, knowing what I know now. What is left to be said when there are at least three members of society who are now dead because of these three men? Did these victims deserve the anger and rage that these men felt they were entitled to take out on another person? Perhaps someone more gracious than you or I can intervene and intercede on behalf of these three men, for whom I pray every day.

And you who were once estranged and hostile in mind, doing evil deeds, he has now reconciled in his fleshly body through death (Colossians 1:21-22).

5. Being Wise as Serpents

There are many serendipitous "ah hah" experiences that a chaplain experiences in prison. One of these came when I was transferred to a minimum-security prison. Peter, one of the chapel workers, kept insisting that he needed to make a phone call from the chapel after the worship service on Sunday evening. Phone calls are discretionary matters that a chaplain is allowed to give on an occasional basis for emergency matters. Peter needed to make these calls in order to clarify some issues with his family.

I did not take much notice of these requests until they became more numerous and more insistent in nature. Peter felt that he was entitled to make these calls. He felt he had the authority to make them as often as was necessary. I found this behaviour odd. At first, I thought it had to do with the more relaxed atmosphere of the lower security facility. It was only as I got to know him better that I realized that Peter was an informant for the institution. He was reporting every activity that happened in the chapel as well as every action I was taking. He felt he was entitled to make any phone call that he wanted because he was doing such a good job for administration.

I learned a valuable lesson. The other inmate chapel workers knew about Peter's clandestine activities. They wanted me to find out "in the worst way." They could not break the "con code" to inform on one of their own. I am sure they prayed that I would find out and that I would not do anything stupid that would get me fired. They hoped that I would find out sooner rather than later about this man's "service for the institution." But they were in danger of backlash if they would "tell on him."

I am grateful today that God gave me a sixth sense that there was something wrong with the picture in front of me. I was able to be more firm with Peter. I was more reflective on the things I was doing right. I was more conscious of the fact that prison can be a very transparent place. People may know everything that is going on in my work. That should be a source of comfort, should it not?

I am not asking you to take them out of the world, but I ask you to protect them from the evil one (John 17:15).

6. *The Cost of Doing What is Right*

An incident occurred in which I had to confront Lyle, one of two chapel workers. Lyle and Richard helped me with worship services and clean-up around the chapel. Lyle was gregarious, involved in music ministry and presided over chapel events. Richard was more soft-spoken, but equally helpful.

I noticed that Richard was becoming more and more withdrawn. He felt inadequate in leading services and was reluctant to come down to the chapel. One day, I asked him about it. Richard told me that there were some things happening that were not appropriate. He showed me a wall cavity in the chapel washroom in which water bottles were being kept, sold and exchanged. These water bottles were filled with home-made brew (alcohol). Richard told me without telling me that it was someone in the chapel who was arranging these exchanges.

I informed the security department about what was happening. They verified that Lyle was involved. They were able to put a stop to the manufacture and distribution of home-made alcohol. What is curious about this event is that the person who told me, Richard, rather than the culprit, ended up in segregation. I inadvertently let it slip to Lyle that it was someone I knew in the chapel who had informed me about this activity. He figured it out and was threatening to injure Richard. Richard asked to stay in segregation because of his fear of Lyle.

Richard thanked me for my ministry when I visited him in the "hole," even though I was responsible for him ending up there. Richard said that it felt good to do something right and to know that Lyle had been caught. This exchange revealed to me that Richard was ready and eager to change. Lyle, on the other hand, had been using the chapel to carry on clandestine activities. He was still wrapped up in his crime cycle. The Bible verse that speaks about "suffering for what is right instead of retaliating" is correct. There is freedom in doing what is right that transcends the suffering that is incurred by "sticking one's neck out."

For it is better to suffer for doing good, if suffering should be God's will, than to suffer for doing evil (1 Peter 3:17).

7. Deportation Orders

One of the realities of the new world order is that many non-citizens are deported from countries in which they have committed a crime. This is the case with many minority offenders with whom I work. For some of them, the only part of Canada they have seen is the airport and the prison. They were convicted of trying to smuggle drugs into the country and sentenced to several years. After serving a certain amount of time in a Canadian prison, they are sent back to their home country.

A small portion of this group has resided in Canada for most of their lives. They are deportable because they or their parents failed to apply for citizenship when they came to Canada. Once these non-citizens have committed a crime and served prison time, they are deported to another country. They then have to wait for five years after their sentences have been completed to apply to immigrate back to Canada.

Steve was part of the latter group. Even though he had lived in Canada since he was four years old, the government was prepared to deport him back to an Eastern European country because of his crimes. Steven was forty years old and had been involved with the justice system for the last twenty years. The only language he knew was English. He had no family in the original country from which he and his parents had come.

When Steve learned that he was going to be deported, he indicated on an "inmate request form" that he was going to kill someone. He did this because he wanted to stay "at home," namely in prison for the rest of his life. Prison life was more real for Steve than any other existence he had ever known. Needless to say, Steve was immediately transferred to a maximum-security prison. Immigration officials communicated with him by tele-conference for the next two years while Steve resisted their attempts to deport him.

I corresponded with an immigration official during this time. I wrote that Steve's situation was different from ninety percent of the cases with which I worked. In spite of his lengthy juvenile and adult record, Steve deserved to be treated as a Canadian citizen. The immigration department eventually agreed. Steve was released to the community. Steve left the prison with gratitude. He made amends to his family with whom he had had brief contact, and continued his life.

You shall also love the stranger, for you were strangers in the land of Egypt (Deuteronomy 10:19).

8. Arctic Adventure

One of my philosophies of ministry comes from an arctic fiction book that I read while in Bible College. Two Inuit men set out on a seal hunt with their dogs, sleds, and boat strapped to their *komatik* (dog sled). Within two days they were on the ice floes and were successful in killing two harp seals. They skinned the seals, ate a sumptuous meal, and settled into their igloo. By the next morning, they found themselves in the middle of a snow storm. After waiting out most of the storm, they set a course for home with the help of their dogs. Unfortunately, the sled went over a sharp ice ridge and came crashing down on its side. The contents were spilled all over the ice and into the water. The men saved what they could and continued, a little wetter, but still optimistic about their prospects.

Unfortunately, they were again forced to set up for the night because of another storm. They stayed in their igloo for the next three days. Finally, the men set out once more. They veered off path because of the breaking up of the ice floes. The men floated along currents that took them in the opposite direction of their settlement. They used their sled and boat for fuel to keep warm. The dogs provided them with some nourishment. The men were finally rescued by a plane that spotted them from overhead. Food was lowered to them, but for some reason no fresh water was supplied. There they were, in the middle of a salt sea, having to wait a little longer before getting much needed water.

Several aspects of the story appeal to my sense of ministry. First, the Inuit hunters remained optimistic throughout the ordeal. They concentrated on what they had left to survive rather than on the obvious trouble they were in. This attitude revealed their courage and fortitude. Secondly, the men improvised and built on the strengths they had learned through earlier hardships. This attitude requires skill and insight. Finally, the rescue was misguided in that it did not provide the nourishment they needed most, fresh water. The hunters had to wait patiently rather than do the desperate thing of drinking the salt water that was all around them.

These virtues of optimism, courage, fortitude, improvisation, and patience have helped prisoners cope in circumstances where there are few pieces left to pick up. Prison is a place where one has to build on the small things that matter. Prison is a place where help can easily become misguided if one does not listen carefully to what is being requested.

We also boast in our sufferings, knowing that suffering produces endurance, and endurance produces character, and character produces hope (Romans 5:3-4).

9. *Nothing but the Love of Jesus*

Visiting the Dissociation and Segregation area of a prison on a regular basis is one of the harder tasks of a chaplain. Going to the "hole" feels a little bit like entering a long dark tunnel from which one may not emerge. Offenders go to D. and S. because they have assaulted another inmate, threatened a guard, are afraid for their lives, owe a lot of money to their fellow offenders, or are unmanageable. I know of several offenders who go from dissociation in one prison to dissociation in another prison without ever spending any length of time in "population." They are not capable of coping with everyday life. I remember making a contract with Ben. He promised that he would try and spend more time in "population." He had lived for over five of the previous nine years in dissociation. Being in the "hole" means being locked up for twenty-three of twenty-four hours a day. There is one hour for recreation, a shower, and perhaps a phone call. A person in that situation can easily lose all sense of reality.

I visited Ken, a young offender in D. and S. who had been in the Young Adult Group that I had facilitated. He had given up his gang affiliation and was committed to changing his life. He was in communication with his girlfriend and two children. He would soon be released into a half-way house in the community. As we met in a small office that doubled as a storage room, Ken saw my supply of Bibles, daily readings, and calendars. He remarked, "Hi chaplain. I see that you have nothing to bring me but the love of Jesus."

He had no idea how true that was. How often I had come to D. and S. with nothing to bring but a soothing word, a word of hope, and a chance to talk about sanity in the midst of insanity. Ken had no idea how helpless I felt. There was little I could do in response to the bizarre behaviours that had led to Ken's sojourn in this dark and dingy place.

All time stops when one sits with *"STORY"* scratched upside down on the metal table in front of you. There is constant shouting in the background. Staff interrupts to get inmate winter jackets. Ken had nothing at all, except the honour of his name itself. That name was now mud because he was an "informer" or could not pay his debts. He was perhaps violent and could not control his temper. What hope could I offer except love itself? Ken recognized this virtue as more concrete than all the walls that were closing in on him, and me.

For God so loved the world that he gave his only Son (John 3:16).

10. The Unintended Consequences of Freedom

A colleague gave me a cartoon some years ago. It showed two tropical fish lying on a table beside an aquarium with a hole cut into the glass. Water was spilling through the hole onto the table and floor. A glass cutter was lying beside one of the fish. The other fish asked, "Now what?"

These two fish had worked toward a short-term goal without considering the larger consequences. Offenders are sometimes like these fish. They want their freedom in the worst way without recognizing the need for water to sustain their existence. Offenders who are released into the community have often worked so hard for their freedom that they have no idea what to do with it once they have it.

The people of Israel during their sojourn in Egypt were in a similar position. Moses had worked so hard for his people's release from Pharaoh that neither he nor the people knew what to do in the wilderness once they got there. Receipt of the Ten Commandments enabled the Israelites to forge themselves into the semblance of a nation. They continued to grumble that they did not have enough "water to live in" to sustain their existence.

Conditions of parole are similar to the Ten Commandments. They list the minimum dos and don'ts of living in the community. These conditions are like a net with large holes in it that is cast into the sea to catch the biggest misdemeanours. They are not meant as a life-line that can sustain a person when meeting one challenge after another. Jesus was right when he said that it is not only an "eye for an eye" that should worry us. Thoughts of killing, lusting, and envying are deadly to one's spirit.

Conversely, love of God in one's heart and casting one's cares upon God provide the greatest returns. Building on the little things, like being thankful for manna and quails, encouraged the Israelites to keep going. Despite the presence of God that threatened to kill them, God provided a cloud of *telos* (goal) that led them to the Promised Land. Similar to the wilderness journey of the Israelites, offenders have to be on the "outside" as long as they have been on the "inside" to get adjusted to what is normal.

As the parent of any teenager knows, freedom from authority is uppermost in a child's mind. It is difficult to concentrate on what is needed to live when one is asserting one's independence. This negative energy can have catastrophic effects, as an offender knows only too well. It takes time to realize that we are our own authority or, shall we say, under God's authority.

I am the Lord your God, who brought you out of the land of Egypt, out of the house of slavery (Exodus 20:2).

11. Too Proud to Beg

There is a famous story about two rich men who have been dispossessed of everything that they own as a result of the Russian Revolution. They are standing on a Moscow street corner. One man takes his hat off, and extends it upside down toward the people passing by. The other man looks at him and asks, "What are you doing?" The first man replies, "What's the matter? Are you too proud to beg?"

This scene came to my mind as I was speaking to Charles, a tall young man who was being released from prison. He told me that he had very little money and no place to go. I suggested to Charles that he could stay at the local Salvation Army hostel. He looked at me in surprise and retorted, "I will never go to a filthy, low-down place like that." With a smile, I replied, "What's the matter? Are you too proud to beg?"

The Harbour Light Mission, the place transients call home, would be better than Charles' current circumstances. He would be free to come and go at the hostel. He would have to pay minimal rent. He could receive help from any one of the dedicated counsellors and volunteers on staff. Unlike the limited amount of options Charles had inside prison, the Mission was a place of opportunity.

Charles acknowledged the weight of my words. Staying at the hostel meant that he might have to admit that he is a transient, without a permanent home. Charles might have to admit that he is an addict who has been unable to control his impulses. He might be at the end of his financial rope and have to ask for social assistance. Charles might be without the emotional know-how to develop meaningful relationships that can sustain him in the long run. Compared to Charles, the destitute rich men in Moscow had everything. They knew what it took to move on.

This is the difference between voluntary and involuntary poverty. Hippies in the 1960s who slept in the streets, hitchhiked across the country, and rubbed shoulders with the less-fortunate knew that they had the means at any time to reclaim the heritage they were rejecting. Many became millionaires in the 70s and 80s. The men beside whom they slept were not as lucky. The hostel for these men was home because they had failed at so many things. They lacked the spiritual and social imagination to move forward. This vacuum of existence is what Charles feared when I suggested that the Mission was a great place to stay.

Blessed are the poor in spirit, for theirs is the kingdom of heaven (Matthew 5:3).

12. Rejected by Society

The extraordinary story of Jean Valjean is recounted in Victor Hugo's novel, Les Miserables. It tells the story of a convict who, after nineteen years of incarceration, is redeemed and transformed by the love of others. Justification occurs when the bishop gives Jean Valjean back the plates and silverware that Jean has stolen. Sanctification occurs when Jean enters surreptitiously into the convent of some nuns and is reformed by their voluntary acts of spiritual discipline.

This riveting story of salvation becomes all the more daunting when, forty pages before the end of the twelve hundred and twenty page book, Jean Valjean is rejected by Marius, his new son-in-law. Jean has just volunteered the fact that he is an ex-convict. Let us listen to Marius' reaction:[16]

"... he (Jean Valjean) was a convict, that is, the creature, who, on the social ladder, has no place, being below the lowest round.... The convict is no longer, so to speak, the fellow of the living. The law has deprived him of all the humanity which it can take from a man.

... He (Marius) thought it natural that certain infractions of the written law should be followed by eternal penalties, and he accepted social damnation as growing out of civilization.

... after having considered Jean Valjean long, his final action was to turn away his head. *Vade retro*."

Marius' act of damnation and denunciation is all the more frightening because this is the first time Jean Valjean has willingly revealed his identity to save himself. Up to this point he has confessed his past in order to save others. Now he has had the courage to believe that his own son-in-law will accept him. This proves to be a false expectation. Jean Valjean is reduced to visiting Cosette, his adopted daughter, once a week in the basement of Marius' upper-middle class home.

The ending of the story is not quite as bad as all this. Marius comes to accept his new father-in-law when he realizes that Jean Valjean saved him from being killed at the barricades. The reader, however, is not quite so forgiving of Marius' response. The excruciating tale of recriminations, self-examinations, transformation of love, and cruel retributions of the book's first thousand pages leaves a person breathless. The *denouement* that occurs at the end does not provide quite enough solace. Victor Hugo understood very well what it was like to be rejected by society.

He was despised and rejected by others; a man of suffering and acquainted with infirmity (Isaiah 53:3).

13. Address Books and Telephone Communication

Prisons are usually built as far away from society as possible. Offenders are literally "put away" because of their crimes. The isolation and alienation that results from this separation causes inmates to cherish each form of communication that they receive. This can take the form of letters, Bible studies, phone calls, and visits.

A reason for communication break-down has to do with the fact that offenders have burnt many bridges. Over fifty percent of my time is spent listening to an inmate grieving the loss of his career, wife, children, and reputation. The loss of hope, love, trust, and faithfulness is a concomitant part of this suffering. Many offenders begin their first interview by speaking about the support they have from their wife and children. In less than a year's time, they come back to tell me they have lost their family. Fear of loss is a big reason why offenders hang on to the smallest scraps of love and attention that they receive from whoever will give it.

Two images come to mind in naming the extent of this alienation. Robin Evans published an article on the inter-relationship between positive and negative energy.[17] In the illustration he placed a large plus (+) sign over the invention of the telephone and a large negative (-) sign over the establishment of the penitentiary. The telephone represents a space-less channel of communication that reaches across vast divides and brings loved ones together. Offenders want to hear the voice of their estranged family members and children. That is why so many of them carry around little red address books that are supplied by a local Gospel Association.

The other image that comes to mind is a movie that I saw in the 1970s. A man moved to Chicago to find work. He carried a picture of his wife and children in his wallet. Every so often he would take out the picture and gaze lovingly at it. This continued throughout the movie. In the closing scene, the man received a phone call. He took the picture out of his wallet and ripped it into a thousand shreds. It was his last link to love, warmth, belonging, and security. Loneliness, despair and self-destruction were all that was left. That final scene touched me as a young man. I was living in the city and finding the adjustment away from family and friends difficult.

Remember that you were at that time without Christ, being aliens from the commonwealth of Israel, and strangers to the covenants of promise, having no hope and without God in the world (Ephesians 2:12).

14. *Tilting Against Windmills*

The above expression comes from a sixteenth-century novel about Don Quixote.[18] Don Quixote is a fanciful old man who imagines himself to be a knight in shining armour going on a chivalrous adventure. As he embarks on this journey, he mistakes a windmill for a walking giant and goes to battle against it. The moral of the story is that we have to know the difference between our imaginary and real enemies to succeed in life.

Discernment of enemies and weighing the cost of fighting against them is something I emphasize to inmates on a daily basis. Tom had confessed to his crime and was convicted of first degree murder. For the next ten years, he appealed his case to the Supreme Court of Canada. He found a reason for living by appealing his conviction. Should I have told him that this might be a case of "tilting against windmills"?

Chaplains are drawn to such cases because there is often a bone of truth among the rags of crime and punishment to be found in prison. I worked in vain with one man, Robert, who I believed was undeserving of his sixteen-year sentence. In spite of all my efforts, Robert completed most of his sentence before being released to the community.

When is it appropriate to tell a man that his case is hopeless and that he will be in jail for the rest of his life? When is it judicious to intervene in a man's ravings and suggest that there are some small steps that he can take to move ahead? A chaplain has to intercept the downward spiral that many offenders have worked themselves into, and offer realistic signs of hope.

Bruno Bettelheim's insight into the difference between fairy tales and myths is instructive.[19] A myth is an epic adventure beyond the normal possibilities of human existence that often ends in failure. Shakespeare's tragedies are examples in this category. Most of the protagonists are lying dead on the stage at the end of the drama. A myth carries a fatalistic, pessimistic end.

By contrast, a fairy tale presents extraordinary opportunities to ordinary people in order to offer the protagonist hope as well as a means to achieve success. In spite of giants who threaten to devour the little child, there is a means of escape at hand. Those are the solutions I look for as a chaplain.

The Philistine said to David, "Am I a dog, that you come to me with sticks?" (I Samuel 17:43)

15. *Living above the Law*

Michael was a relatively good looking, forty-year old man. He sat in my office with a newspaper open in front of him. He had just received a sixteen year sentence for laundering money for a criminal organization. Michael had a Master of Arts degree in psychology and could analyse people along with the best program facilitators in the institution. He sat there, justifying himself without admitting his involvement. He remarked, "Sometimes a person has to live above the law."

That remark was chilling. Colombian drug warlords had just destabilized their government by shooting federal judges who were prosecuting their gang. A Montreal defence lawyer had just been shot dead while parked at a stop sign in an upper-middle class neighbourhood. A motorcyclist had recently followed a provincial guard home after her late night shift and shot her. A gun-man had opened fire at six o'clock in the morning on a federal van that was escorting two prisoners to court. Local criminal organizations were intimidating anyone who was trying to bring them to justice. Their strategy appeared to be working. The gangs were becoming brazen and desperate enough to attack federal agents openly.

My responsibilities as a chaplain included offering religious services to Michael. I had cause to pause that day and wonder if I was doing any good. I could only be appalled at the amount of power this man's criminal organization had inside and outside of prison. Attempts to kill inmates who spoke up against this situation were blatant. What possible role could a chaplain have in light of these decidedly wicked endeavours?

I gained a new appreciation for the difficulties in which the government is involved in bringing criminals to justice. The criminal organizations' devious attempts to "live beyond the law" can only be matched by the wits, cunning, strategies, and commitment of the justice department. I realized that my role as a chaplain had as much to do with pointing out the errors of Michael's ways as with providing a safe haven for his lack of remorse.

For the wrath of God is revealed from heaven against all ungodliness (Romans 1:18).

16. Burying One's Loved Ones in the Church Cemetery

After years of indecision, a Catholic priest in the Hamilton area stood up to the Italian Mafia members of his church and refused to bury one of their own in the church cemetery. He declared that the criminal behaviour of the dead man did not square with the religious piety that the man had exhibited. The priest could not in good conscience give him a religious burial with all the eternal blessings that such a gesture would imply.

This announcement took a lot of courage. Italian members of the Mafia are notoriously ruthless in their dealings with anyone who crosses their paths. Their wanton disregard for others is matched by their deep religiosity and sense of belonging within the Catholic Church. I remember an eighty-five year-old mother of a sixty year-old offender named Tony attending a family social in the prison chapel. His mother was dressed from head to toe in her black Sunday best, veil included. Tony gave long accounts of helping out in a senior citizen home while on day parole. I could only marvel at the incongruity of the picture before me.

I realized that everyone wants to be blessed. Tony wanted to feel justification for his life if not for his crime. He wanted to be absolved and consecrated even though he continued in whatever way possible to rationalize his criminal actions. I was to provide that blessing, even though my conscience rebelled against the idea of it.

Mafia criminal mores are nurtured within a familial and religious milieu. This creates an aura of legitimation that belies the evil nature of their criminal actions. I remember when a new grocery store was built in my neighbourhood. I spoke about this new enterprise to Stephano, the barber who was cutting my hair. He casually remarked, "It is too bad that this store was allowed to move into the area. This places too much competition on the grocery chain that is already here. This would not have been allowed in the good old days when the community had better control of the situation."

This remark was a veiled reference to the power that the crime syndicate used to exert against any new competition in the neighbourhood. This casual remark revealed to me how well a crime organization can hide behind ordinary business ventures.

He did what was evil in the sight of the Lord; he did not depart all his days from any of the sins of Jeroboam son of Nebat (2 Kings 15:18).

17. People of the Lie

Scott Peck, in his acclaimed book, People of the Lie,[20] tells the story of a couple who gave their oldest son a .22-calibre rifle for his birthday. He ended up committing suicide by shooting himself with this rifle. While going through the normal grieving process, the parents did not know what to do with the gun. They gave it to their next oldest son, who was fourteen.

Peck is amazed that the parents did not know what message they were sending to their younger son. They were showing their lack of love for their second son by asking him (subconsciously) to do the same thing that his older brother had done. They did not appear to want to have children. They were conveniently getting rid of them by having them commit suicide.

Peck's point is that the intentions of our heart are sometimes evident to other people while remaining hidden from ourselves. This is a situation that I frequently encounter when I interview inmates. Their high-speed car chases, near-death experiences, drug use, and "devil-may-care" attitude are the direct result of traumatic events in their lives. In Adam's case, his mother's banishment of him to foster care at the age of twelve led to his acting out. Nick used the fact that he could not go to his father's funeral while incarcerated to justify his next crime. The unfaithfulness of Tanner's wife led him to seek love in other places.

These men became aware of cause-and-effect relationships as they spent time in jail. Adam realized he had a lot of hatred and resentment toward his mother. He had always referred to her as a "saint." Tanner realized that he still cared for his wife in spite of the isolation and separation that had occurred over several years. Tanner and Adam began to own the reality of the situation that was once veiled to them.

These contributing factors do not justify the severe harm that Adam and Tanner caused others. The self-revelations nevertheless go a long way in helping these young men understand the reasons for their actions. It is within the safety and nurture of a chaplain's office that these deep-seated issues can come to the fore. Confessing wrongs to another person goes a long way toward bringing comfort to a very sad situation.

Lord, if you choose, you can make me clean (Luke 5:12).

18. "When I was Five Years Old"

An offender by the name of Kevin threatened a staff member and ended up in segregation as a result of the risk of his violence. The following day, Kevin sent me a five page yellow-foolscap journal. He described how he had to "threaten someone" so that he could get his "forty days and nights" in the wilderness with Jesus and Moses.

I was at a loss how to work with this man. Kevin's long scriptural tirades combined with his emotional instability and poor coping skills made me wonder how I could help. I did not want to enable him by adding more scriptural reflections to his already large bonfire of beliefs. I was not a psychologist equipped with knowledge of behavioural patterns. I was not a psychiatrist who could prescribe medications to balance this man's emotional highs and lows.

This problem was solved for me within ten minutes of our conversation in the "hole." Midway through a discussion in which Kevin and I were talking about a salient point of scripture, I touched a nerve. Kevin responded, "When I was five years old . . ." At that moment all time stopped. I realized we were talking about something real, so real that this recalled moment of forty years ago had come to define the very being of this man.

We never had to speak of scriptures again. We could mutually "own" the experience of abuse by a priest that had come to shape Kevin's emotional and social turmoil. No more boasting about gang affiliations. No more threats of violence. No more speeches about heroic deeds of misplaced bravado. Kevin was able to describe his rage at life because of what this "man of God" had done to him at a young age. We could speak about hurt and pain. We could cry a little. I could own the anger that Kevin felt against the priest. I as a chaplain literally "stood in" for what this priest had done. No amount of explanation could undo the pain that had been suffered. A sense of forgiveness on the victim's part for what had happened to him so many years ago was present in the room that day.

I never had to wonder again whether I could work with Kevin. In spite of his continued flare ups, tantrums, and paranoia, I knew that Kevin was working sincerely on his life and future. He was able to face his demons. Six years later, Kevin is still in the community. He has been able — with the help of many people — to find a way beyond the morass of street life and remand centers to something he can call family.

Before I formed you in the womb I knew you, and before you were born I consecrated you (Jeremiah 1:5).

19. Attracted to the Infamous

A newspaper article reported that a pastor from a local city was the first witness at the fifteen-year judicial review of a high profile offender. The pastor testified how the convicted person had given his life to Jesus and was a born-again believer. The article went on to note that the offender continued to claim his innocence. This denial of guilt flew in the face of a lot of evidence at the trial.

This incident made me realize two things. First, chaplains and volunteers alike are attracted to infamous offenders. These offenders are often the most "pro-social," the most "like us," the most "different," or the most "fascinating." I remember a drug dealer who told me that he turned to crime because he did not get a million dollar contract for his construction company. He had wanted to become famous. Now he was infamous.

There is something about the most heinous of crimes that makes us want to "figure out" what makes that person tick. Countless television programs analyse criminal intent. These parallel the health shows that try to figure out why a person is sick.

Part of our attraction to infamous offenders comes from our need to prove that God can change the worst sinners. Transformation is not valid unless there has been a great deal of sin. This is why evangelical conversion stories are so compelling. If God can change these men, then there is hope for us. We get caught up in the emotional roller-coaster ride of faith because of our own doubts about God's acceptance.

The newspaper article also made me realize that actual transformation is not always evident. The pathological nature of the offender or the irretrievable truth of the offence makes any real reconciliation among the parties concerned difficult. The facts and forgiveness of the matter may have to be taken to the grave. This cold eventuality does not bring relief to the victims. I remember a victim who was interviewed after the killer of his child had been executed. The interviewer asked, "Are you satisfied?" "No" was the reply.

God has forgiven a person. We, however, may not be able to forgive that person. The sheer gravity of the situation flies in the face of everything we know. Is that why we are so attracted to the infamous?

Father, forgive them; for they do not know what they are doing (Luke 23:34).

20. Psalm 91:7

I was taken aback when I saw "Psalm 91:7" etched as a tattoo across an inmate's back. It was hard for me to imagine why a person would write a Bible verse in ink on his body. I consulted my Bible and came across these words:

A thousand may fall at your side,
Ten thousand at your right hand,
But it will not come near you.

The inmate had seen so many of his gang comrades killed that he wanted to make sure that God kept him alive. He took God's promises literally when God said that the angels will protect him and that the arrows of the enemy will miss him.

A similar theme of invincibility appears in the first *Matrix* movie. The chief protagonist dodges bullets and miraculously rises from the dead at the end of the movie. Many of the men with whom I work loved the movie. They believe that they are invincible because they are still alive. They have lived to tell the tale of car crashes, drive-by shootings, beatings, and stabbings. Only God knows why they have been kept alive. God must have a greater purpose for their lives.

The Glory and Praise hymn book includes a song based on Psalm 91:7 entitled, "Blest be the Lord." It says we have nothing to fear because of our faith in God. We can claim the victory God has granted to us.

I am not sure when I sing this song if God is going to keep these men alive. Some members of the congregation have killed rival gang members. They have "ratted out" their bosses. They have severely harmed family members. There are contracts out on some of these men's lives. Some of them are afraid to go home for a family member's funeral because a sniper may be lying in wait. There are good reasons why this song is so meaningful:

Refrain
Blest be the Lord, blest be the Lord, the God of mercy, the God who saves.
I shall not fear the dark of night, nor the arrow that flies by day.

Verse 1
He will release me from the nets of all my foes,
He will protect me from their wicked hands.
Beneath the shadow of His wings I will rejoice
To find a dwelling place secure.[21]

21. Keeping a Clock on a Wall

The office I shared with another chaplain was almost completely bare. There was a single picture of Jesus on the wall. The desks were uncluttered, with almost nothing in the drawers. I had just arrived at the institution and was not sure what to make of the situation.

I brought several things from home to make the office more inviting. I put a clock on the wall. I put some books on the shelves. I found a comfortable sofa on which inmates could sit. As I settled into my office chair, the chapel cleaner came into the room. He looked around at the new arrangement and commented, "That clock is not going to stay there."

The reason he knew so much was because he was the one who had pilfered everything of use in the office. The other chaplain had become tired of trying to change the stealing habits of his parishioners. He kept the office bare enough so that there was little left to take.

I took a different tack. I told the worker that the clock was intended to stay there. I told him that I expected him to make sure it did. We did not have any problems. Before long, I brought in some inexpensive works of art, put up a tack board, and continued in a reasonably comfortable fashion.

We all get to the end of our ropes. There are so many demands in our jobs. We endure so much disrespect of our roles and so much questioning of our authority that we keep the cupboards of our souls bare. There is little left to steal when we have left the care of our ministry at the door of the prison. This is when we know that we need help. How can we replenish the resourcefulness of our hearts?

New volunteers have a favourite saying. "I have received more from the offenders than I have given them." This saying sounds hollow when repeated a hundred times after ten years of ministry. The truth of the matter is that many of us as pastors and priests and chaplains and volunteers "have given and given until it hurts." Ministry can easily become a one-way street in which inmates expect us to have an endless resource of spiritual wealth to share. We are the ones who are expected to set limits on our care, rather than the other way around. When will the internal checkpoint of inmates provide a safe space in which chaplains and offenders can establish a mutual relationship of respect and encouragement?

This is why keeping the clock on the wall is so important. There are reasonable standards of conduct to which all of us need to adhere. There is inherent respect for the chapel that has to be safeguarded in order for worship to take place. Spiritual health enables us to work for the glory of God.

I am grateful to Christ Jesus our Lord, who has strengthened me (1 Timothy 1:12).

- Chapter Two -

Marriage and Parenting

1. Marriage and the Correctional Investigator

It is not often that one gets a phone call from the correctional investigator. The correctional investigator is a person in the Service who is responsible for answering grievances that offenders make against staff. He or she tries to sort out the problem and negotiate a satisfying settlement.

I got a call from this person because I had refused to marry one of the offenders and his fiancée. Civil marriages were not allowed in prison until 1991. The only way an offender could get married was through the auspices of the Protestant chaplain. The Catholic Church in the region where I worked rarely performed marriages in prison. There were various reasons for this. First, prison was not considered a public place where wedding banns could be published. No one objecting to the marriage could come and intercede. Secondly, church registries were kept in the parish church and could not be moved without special dispensation. Lastly, marriage was considered a sacrament in the Catholic Church and not to be taken lightly.

I as the Protestant chaplain received a lot of requests for marriages because of these strictures. I facilitated one marriage when a local United Church minister agreed to come in and marry the couple. I facilitated another marriage by accompanying the groom to a local Spanish church. Mario was baptized on the same day so that he could become a member of the church. He was then eligible to be married by the Pentecostal minister. Most other requests I refused because they were a matter of expediency.

I found my hesitancy regarding this matter to be a good thing. It made the couple ponder the reasons for their request. It provided me with the opportunity to work with the couple in marriage preparation. I worked with about seven couples during this time. Several decided that it would be best to remain friends. One partner was pushing for marriage because of his insecurities about his girlfriend's faithfulness. One inmate was tempted by another female friend. He thought this temptation would go away if he married his fiancée. The other couples with whom I worked eventually married and became lifelong partners.

The involuntary strictures of prison have the unintended good effect of making both partners think through the reasons why they want to get married in the first place. I do not know if I was able to satisfy the correctional investigator with this approach. These limitations helped me think more deeply about what marriage means to me.

Therefore a man leaves his father and his mother and clings to his wife, and they become one flesh (Genesis 2:24).

2. Marriages Made in Heaven

The lack of connection between an offender's view of life and reality itself was evident when several volunteers, offenders, and I were sitting around a table engaged in a Bible study. All of them were asked to share their views of marriage. Jeff, an offender whom I knew reasonably well, spoke about how much he believed in marriage. He had a wife and two children and recently had been in contact with them. It sounded as though this match was made in heaven.

These comments struck me because Jeff was actually on his third marriage. He had not been in contact with his children for many years. He had sold all of the furniture for drugs the last time he was with his wife. The only reason Jeff had recent contact with his wife was because she was going to throw away the remains of his personal effects. Before she threw them out, she phoned the institution to see what Jeff wanted to do with them. I was the one who picked up these last mementoes from her place. There was nothing of value in the old ragged suitcase except an old razor, some shaving cream, two old shirts, and some other junk.

Jeff made me understand one thing: even though Jeff's marriage was going badly, he believed in love, marriage, and God. Fantasies of life and faith are powerful sustainers when we are in a vacuous state of flux and clairvoyance. Jeff was really trying to tell us that he wished he had a wonderful marriage. He wished he was not an addict. He wished he could straighten out his life. And Jeff wished the volunteers and chaplain would accept him for who he wanted to be instead of who he was. He had little ability to face the fact that he had a thirty-year old son with his first wife whom he had not seen for twenty-nine years.

There is a happy and sad ending to this story. Jeff was released two years later. He was able to stay clean in the community for three years. He re-connected with his first wife and met his grown son. He was able to be a father to his child and husband to his wife. Sadly, he went back to jail shortly after this period of time. I heard recently that he died in prison. While there, Jeff shared many of his poems in the worship services. He led the chapel choir. He had a gentle spirit that endeared him to all. May he rest in peace!

Let marriage be held in honour by all, and let the marriage bed be kept undefiled (Hebrews 13:4).

3. The Weird and the Wonderful

A fellow chaplain once remarked that prison marriages are like meeting the weird and the wonderful. "One is never sure which is which, but it is always interesting." This proved especially true for the first two weddings in which I was involved. A woman named Genny started corresponding with an offender named Bill through a pen pal program. They fell in love and got married within a year of becoming acquainted. The fact that Genny was handicapped made this relationship exceptional. An even more amazing fact was that within five years of marriage, she was able to conceive and have a baby.

In the second marriage in which I was involved, I asked for references as part of the marriage preparation course. The letter of reference that Tammy, the young fiancée, gave me turned out to be from Chris, a minister whom I knew fairly well. Chris felt that there were good reasons to end the relationship. This information caused quite a bit of consternation on the part of Tammy. We had several more sessions to deal with the issue. In the end, the wedding went ahead, and the marriage proceeded on course.

These examples demonstrate how couples are attracted to each other because of deep wounds they subconsciously recognize in the other person. This fact has been elaborated in a wonderfully redemptive book entitled, Getting the Love You Want, by Harville Hendrix.[22] He suggests that "falling in love at first sight" happens because people recognize something in the other person that needs healing in themselves. Hendrix shows how the married couple spends the rest of their lives balancing their willingness to "save the other person" with the need to be "saved themselves."[23]

Genny and Bill were attracted to each other because of their similar situations. While Bill was working on his parole, Genny was becoming more independent in her living arrangements. She was able to get an apartment on her own as a result of Bill's encouragement. They raised a child together. Tammy was attracted to her prison boyfriend because of the dysfunctional relationships she had had. With the help of her pastor, she saw the reasons for their mutual attraction. Tammy came to terms with the life challenges her boyfriend was facing while being incarcerated.

Hendrix shows how a partner begins to resent the attractive part of a spouse's personality as the marriage proceeds.[24] Each person needs to own the shadow side of one's character in order for the relationship to work.

For the wife does not have authority over her own body, but the husband does; likewise the husband does not have authority over his own body, but the wife does (1 Corinthians 7:4).

4. The Decline and Fall of American Beauty

I found the movie, *American Beauty*, disturbing. Its blatant disrespect for the nuclear family and violent solution to dysfunctional relationships are troublesome. The movie depicts a middle-age couple whose marriage is rapidly dissolving. Faced with work pressures, the husband quits his job and works for $5/hour at a fast-food restaurant. Disillusioned with her husband, the wife commits adultery with her colleague.

The odd behaviour of their children is a natural outcome of these marriage woes. The daughter demonstrates her emotional turmoil through her black wardrobe and disgust at her father's infatuation with her teenage friend. The son finds an outlet in voyeuristic photography.

This story is further complicated by the depiction of a repressed homosexual military officer who mercilessly disciplines his own son. His son acts out by dealing drugs and becoming anti-social.

Each of these situations is redeemable from a pastoral point of view. The couple could acknowledge the tragedy of their marriage and become reconciled or get a divorce. The daughter could confront her father over his inappropriate fantasies. The son could be helped with his exhibitionistic tendencies by establishing pro-social relationships. The military officer could own his repressed desires. And his son could be counselled in terms of job skills and need for independence from his father.

The movie chooses instead to opt for a violent ending. The military officer kills the father because of a perceived homosexual liaison between the father and the military officer's son. Meanwhile, the wife is firing guns at a local gun club with her real-estate lover. Their teenagers are handling guns as they talk about their disgust for their parents.

These scenarios are all too real for me. I work with men who have killed their parents and siblings. I work with repressed men who have sexually abused children to satisfy their fantasies. I work with gay men who are struggling with their identity. And I work with anti-social persons who deal drugs and act out in any number of inappropriate ways.

I ask myself: Why are these taboos celebrated in *American Beauty*? Have we gone beyond good and evil, as Frank Coppola's movie about the Vietnam War, *Apocalypse Now,* suggests? Why did the movie not attempt to come up with more reasonable ways of solving difficult relationships?

Do you not know that you are God's temple and that God's Spirit dwells in you? (1 Corinthians 3:16).

5. *Why Did I Ever Get Married?*

One of the best alternatives to *American Beauty* is the relatively recent movie, *Why Did I Ever Get Married?*, by director Tyler Perry. It depicts four couples who are facing serious marriage problems. One spouse is blaming the other for the death of their daughter in an accident. Both spouses in another marriage are having affairs. Another spouse continually ridicules his wife because she is too fat. And the fourth spouse wants his wife to have a child while she wants to stay focused on her career.

The movie offers redemption, reconciliation and relief through confession, dialogue, forgiveness, faith and sharing. Blame is owned and let go of in the case of the dead daughter. Resentment over his wife's career is acknowledged by the husband. The selfishness of another couple is revealed as they confess their two affairs. The fourth marriage is dissolved when the wife realizes that her obedient submissiveness has resulted in abuse by her husband and low self-esteem on her part. She learns to carry on with faith, to the ultimate regret and chagrin of her estranged husband.

The movie is redeeming because it offers honest solutions to the most pernicious marriage problems. The divorced man acknowledges that his pretty new young bride is only worth twenty percent of what his first, loving and faithful wife gave to him over many years. The estranged wife realizes that her overly devout faith compensated for her bad marriage. It contributed to her inappropriate submissiveness. She learns to validate herself through God's eyes with the help of a new friend.

Three of the four couples are vulnerable enough to realize that their marriages are doomed unless they take a radically different approach. Each of them struggles to a joyous reclamation of their love for each other.

The genius of the movie lies in its unapologetic, yet unobtrusive use of faith, prayer, worship, and church membership. Faith is depicted as a normal part of life that can be brought to bear on one's problems. Even though sin is an inevitable reality of life, it reminds us that we as Christians have a choice and an opportunity to rectify the situation. Perry's movies shine with a brilliant radiance of transformation that is hard to pinpoint. This type of effervescence is what we need to feel and experience in our work as prison chaplains.

Therefore, let us celebrate the festival, not with the old yeast, the yeast of malice and evil, but with the unleavened bread of sincerity and truth (1 Corinthians 5:8).

6. Saviour Figures in Search of Relationships

Offenders come into my office and talk about the reasons for their return to prison. More often than not, they fell in love with a woman and became intimately involved. They have had to deal with the fall-out as they realized that this match was not made in heaven. Frequently, the man sees himself as a saviour figure that needs to rescue his girl-friend from the dilemmas in which she is mired.

Nathan fell in love with Susanna, a single mother with three children. He could not understand why, after three months, he fled the area and started using drugs in a nearby town. He could not face the responsibility of caring for this family.

Graham had to rescue his younger brother Anthony from the hands of a gang on the first day of his parole. They were threatening to beat Anthony up because he had stolen ten cell phones from them. On the second day of his parole, Graham had to rescue his girlfriend from some men who were threatening to assault her at a drunken party in the middle of the night.

Jessie fell in love with Miranda and got her pregnant. After deciding to keep the baby, Miranda used up all of Jessie's money and then "ditched him" for another man.

Serge fell in love with Nicole, who was quite a bit younger than he. Although Serge was emotionally ready to become attached, Nicole was just starting to discover what it meant to be in love. The relationship fell apart when Serge realized that Nicole could not remain faithful to him.

These cases demonstrate how easy it is to become a saviour figure. These men were attracted to these women because of their own woundedness. They soon discovered that the emotional baggage of their girlfriends was too much for their fragile egos. What first looked attractive became disastrous as the men reverted to their poor coping skills in the face of crises. There were significant consequences to each of the situations mentioned above. The women were left to take care of a new-born baby or simply confused about what had happened. The men were suspended and sent back to jail for parole violations. The men had to start proving their credibility all over again.

When I became an adult, I put an end to childish ways (1 Corinthians 13:11b).

7. Other People's Ways of Parenting

At my best, parenting includes verbal communication and time-outs, along with further explanations and re-assurances. This approach is not embraced by all. Older offenders are used to a quite different method when it comes to dealing with their younger peers. These young adults often act like "punks" who respect neither themselves nor the world around them.

This alternate approach became clear to me when Alfred, an older offender working as a chapel cleaner, approached me. He told me that two younger guys were picking on him. Brian and John would not leave him alone. They were throwing things at him and enjoying the misery it was causing him. Alfred came to me because he was afraid of what he would do if he retaliated.

I suggested that we hold a mediation session among these three men. I had no idea what I was in for. Brian's friend, John, sat in a chair by the window. Alfred sat on a couch on the other end of the room. Brian, the young offender, occupied the chaplain's office chair. I introduced the three men to each other and explained the nature of the problem. I asked Alfred to express his feelings toward the two younger men who had been picking on him. Alfred stood up, put his nose two inches away from Brian's face, and started screaming at him. I was sure at that moment that Brian, along with his friend, John, would get up and "paste" Alfred. Instead, Brian sat there, not saying a word. After the harangue had stopped, Brian acknowledged that he and John had been bullying the older man. Brian promised never to do it again. There were never any more problems among these three men.

I learned that my form of parenting was not the only effective one. The older gentleman had learned a very different style of parenting. Surprisingly, it was one that the younger man was very familiar with. This form of "discipline" was normal in their "world." Harsh words, harsh punishments, bullying and being bullied, along with passive/aggressive behaviours appeared normal. Brian could hear what Alfred was saying. He had trouble following my directions when I spoke more softly.

Hear instruction and be wise (Proverbs 8:33).

8. Nature versus Nurture

One afternoon I received a call from the distraught mother of her adopted son, Jamie. She had just finished visiting him in prison. She was calling to get some advice. She told me, "When I was growing up, I was told that ninety percent of parenting consists of nurturing one's children. The other ten percent has to do with the way one was born. I raised Jamie in exactly the same way as my other three children. My other children are law-abiding citizens, while Jamie has been in and out of prison for the last twenty years. It should be the other way around. Ninety percent of one's character has to do with nature, while ten percent has to do with nurture."

I knew that Jamie was struggling to live up to his adopted parents' expectations. He had his own issues of identity, abandonment, and addictions to deal with. He felt loved and accepted by his adopted family, even though he could not explain why he had turned out so differently. The last I heard, he was staying committed to his recently proclaimed Christian faith, had forgiven himself, was accepting his serious health issues, and was working on release plans into the community.

I agree with the sentiments of Jamie's mother. The young men with whom I work are much closer in character and life-style to their parents than they would care to admit. The trick is to get them to speak about their upbringing in order for them to reflect on the ways that they are the same as their parents. For some, their drug of choice is cocaine instead of the alcoholism of their mother. For others, their crime is selling drugs instead of their father's spousal abuse. For still others, there was so little parenting at home that their group-home peers were the ones who got them hooked on stealing. The initial neglect and abuse was masked and transformed into something else in order for the young men to claim that they were different from their parents.

"There is no way," Jordan retorted, "that I would ever drink alcohol or beat my wife. I experienced that in my home. I have been cured of that forever." That statement was true. And yet, here Jordan was, sitting in jail, having murdered someone for a drug heist gone wrong. The initial issues simply resurfaced in other ways.

The fact that we live in response to the preoccupations of our parents needs further reflection. We need to recognize that we are preoccupied in a similar manner, but with a different agenda in mind. Our task is to own parental similarity in order to move beyond it.

Train children in the right way, and . . . they will not stray (Proverbs 22:6).

9. Is History Destined to Repeat Itself?

One of the sad realities of prison life is that young offenders are often more like their fathers than they would care to admit. This fact became abundantly clear to me one evening as I was discussing parenting in the Young Adult Group. I had added the topic after I found out that over half of the twenty-year-olds I was teaching were fathers.

The young men were very good at avoiding the topic. For over an hour, they found ways of speaking about relationships, girlfriends, family, and friends while carefully sidestepping their own involvement as fathers. Exasperated, I asked the group why it was so difficult for them to speak about their role as parents. Alex replied, "Our fathers abandoned us when we were small. Now we are doing the same thing to our children by coming to jail. We are very ashamed of this fact. It is difficult for us to acknowledge and accept our failure as fathers."

What a statement! How ashamed we are of repeating the same mistakes that our parents have made. This is what Alex expressed in his feelings about himself. He realized that even though he hated his unknown father, he had turned out exactly like him. He did not even know how to be and act like a father. Alex felt especially helpless in this situation.

I spoke about the ways the young men could foster emotional and social ties with their children even if they were unable to care for them. Their children still wanted to know whether their young fathers loved them. The children may feel that they are somehow to blame for "Daddy going away." I recommended that any form of communication, however insignificant, should be nurtured in order for their identity as fathers to grow.

Is history destined to repeat itself without hope of liberation from this "rotating wheel of suffering"? Some aspects of Hinduism and Christianity tend toward this sense of fatedness. This view suggests:

"We are pre-destined to turn out a certain way. There is no sense in railing against this fact. One should accept one's station in life and one's place within the hierarchy of matter. We are 'thrown into existence' (Heidegger) without the possibility of making any real choices."[25]

I advise offenders to "own" the fact that they are in jail, that they are experiencing many losses, and that they may never see their children again. Am I unconsciously reinforcing a resigned view of life that has more to do with grieving and consolation than hope and reconciliation?

He will turn the hearts of parents to their children and the hearts of children to their parents (Malachi 4:6).

10. The Prince of Egypt

There is a point in the movie, *The Prince of Egypt*, when a dual image of Moses as Pharaoh and Moses as Israelite appears on the screen. This image slowly divides into two as Moses learns that he was born an Israelite and adopted as Pharaoh's son. Moses visits the tombs of the Pharaohs to learn more about his past. He sees the painting of baby Jews being thrown into the sea at the time of his birth. These brutal acts of his step-father come as a shock. Moses realizes that the pyramids are being built on the backs of his own people. This searing recognition of his past prompts Moses to kill a security guard, run away, and eventually return to oppose the new Pharaoh. The new king turns out to be the person with whom he grew up, his step-brother.

Moses' decision to side with his biological past is gut-wrenching. He is the favoured son of Pharaoh and in line for the throne. Moses is first and foremost a Prince of Egypt who has all the privileges to lead a rich and pampered life. Instead, he becomes a criminal, escaped fugitive, and volunteer slave to help his fellow brothers and sisters. Moses gives up his status because his very birth was shaped by the violence, cruelty and death that his step-father inflicted on his mother's people. Moses has to go beyond the memory of his current life as Pharaoh's favourite son to claim the deep-seated sacrifice that his mother made to save his life.

This story is powerful because so many offenders are step-children who have no idea why they are so dysfunctional in the light of a good foster-care upbringing. The answer is that they are more like their "drunken father" than the people they call Mom and Dad. They are like their neglectful biological parent in their abandonment of their own children. They are like their father who was unable to keep a job. Like Moses, their salvation lies in claiming this hurtful, demeaning past. Owning the "violence" in which they were born paradoxically helps them move beyond it. This is a tragic ownership. The offender has to acknowledge a negative past in order to be saved from repeating it.

For those who want to save their life will lose it, and those who lose their life for my sake will find it. For what will it profit them if they gain the whole world but forfeit their life? (Matthew 16:25-26)

11. Becoming a Foster Parent

The *Blues Brothers 2000* movie is pertinent to chaplaincy for a number of reasons. First, the movie is dedicated to John Belushi, who died of a drug overdose after starring in the first 1982 *Blues Brothers* movie. The second reason is that the movie opens with Elroy (Dan Ackroyd) standing in front of a prison waiting for John Belushi to be released. After waiting a whole night, the warden goes downstairs and tells Elroy that Belushi has died. The third reason is that the nun who raised Elroy as an orphan asks him to "mentor" a young boy who is causing problems in the orphanage. Elroy takes the adolescent under his wing. He is eventually accused of kidnapping him. They end up riding into the sunset with cop cars following behind.

The moral of the story appears to be that even a shady character such as Elroy can learn to be a good parent. The young boy steals money from a head sergeant at the beginning of the movie. This money is used to put the band back together. As Elroy tours the country in search of his old music friends, the adolescent teenager becomes more and more a part of the band. He learns to play the harmonica and is accepted as a son and family member. The "band" serves as a substitute community through which Elroy and the boy find their calling in life. Elroy learns to take responsibility for his newly adopted son.

Christians who watch the movie may have questions about the way in which this parental theme is developed. I would suggest that this movie is appropriate in its redemptive yearnings within difficult circumstances. The movie's mentoring program is aimed directly at the tragedy that was John Belushi's life. Our job, like that of Elroy, is to provide safe environments for young men so that they can make the right choices before it is too late.

For the measure you give will be the measure you get back (Luke 6:38).

- Chapter Three -

Issues of Authority

1. Human versus Divine Authority

One of the first sermons I preached in a medium-security prison was on the difference between human and divine authority. I based my meditation on the relative height of the chapel steeple vis-à-vis the guard tower situated thirty yards away. I asked the offenders which structure was higher. After going outside to check, they verified that the guard tower was higher.

My point was to undergird the amount of human authority that comes into play in a prison atmosphere. The offenders are guarded on a twenty-four hour basis. There are constant passes to be filled out in order for inmates to proceed from one place to another. There are four counts a day in which offenders are locked in their cells to make sure no one has escaped. There are changes of routine at a moment's notice. Searches are intrusive in the sense that everything in a cell can be turned upside down. Disobeying a direct order can have one placed in segregation. Offenders live in fear of being attacked by their peers.

Chaplains are subject to bureaucracy and red tape in the fulfillment of their tasks. The institution is run as a military operation in which each staff member is accountable to the next level of authority. There is a chain of command that staff and offenders follow in order to function well within a prison culture.

Some offenders felt that I was emphasizing human authority to the exclusion of the liberating power of the gospel. I pointed out that prisons were created by society to punish people who have broken human laws. Acquiescence, acceptance, submission, and internalization of human authority go hand in hand with divine intervention. I suggested that it is precisely within the role of human authority that divine sovereignty comes into play.

This is a hard lesson to learn. Many offenders have experienced only the negative use of power. They have thrown out the legitimate baby of human authority with the dirty bathwater of injustice, righteous indignation, oppression, and misguided direction. They rail against the sinful abuse of human power to the exclusion of everything else. This spiritual one-up-man-ship sometimes lands offenders in more trouble than they started with. The challenge is to know how the Holy Spirit can work in wonderful ways through human authority, including the church and prison.

Let every person be subject to the governing authorities (Romans 13:1).

2. Following in the Steps of a Mentor

Chaplain Tilman, who mentored me when I started working in a maximum-security prison, was concerned that I might do something wrong. He had good reason to worry. I was relatively young, did not know a word of French, had no idea of what I was getting into, and knew more about academia and the Bible than about criminology and the prison system.

Needless to say, I learned quickly. I noticed that Tilman would spend an inordinate amount of time checking with each level of authority to get something approved. We went from the keeper to the deputy warden to the preventive security department to the admissions and discharge department to clarify the procedure of getting my security clearance and photo identification. I noticed how important it was to acknowledge each staff member's level of responsibility and authority. They appreciated the fact that the senior chaplain took time to talk to them. Respect was gained on both sides. I realized afterward that this was done for my benefit.

During the week one of the offenders came to Chaplain Tilman's office, upset about something that Tilman had said or done. Tilman took it in stride and spent at least twenty minutes standing toe to toe with the man. Tilman quietly explained the reasons for his actions and the options that were available to them for future meetings. The man's posture slowly relaxed and they were able to come to some mutual agreement. I learned from this experience that I would be dealing directly with many different types of people. I would have to answer honestly and truthfully about my actions and decisions.

Another incident happened during the Sunday evening chapel service over which Tilman presided. I could feel the tension in the room as about twenty offenders and four volunteers gathered in the relatively small space. Halfway through the service, an offender who was leaning against the back wall threw a roll of toilet paper toward the front of the chapel. Tilman stopped the service. He asked whether he would have to call security to deal with the situation. There were several "boos" all around, but the men quieted down after that. As we left for the parking lot that evening, Tilman acknowledged that he might have defused the situation differently. I learned from this incident that I had to be prepared for many different situations. I had to learn to master my fears and not be intimidated.

Do not fear, for I am with you, do not be afraid, for I am your God (Isaiah 41:10).

3. Setting the Agenda

I was asked in an interview for a chaplaincy position how I would minister to offenders. I replied by saying that it was important to listen to the life experiences of an inmate and understand what he felt the needs of his situation to be. One of the interviewers asked about the ministry that I could provide the person. Puzzled by the question, I repeated myself by saying that I would listen carefully to what the person had to say in order to understand the basis of his or her query. It was only later that I realized the interviewer was asking me about the type of gospel, salvation, hope, grace, love, and care I could offer in my ministry.

I wondered why I had made so much of the prisoner as the subject of the sentence. Why was I unable to respond with an action-word or deed that transformed the prisoner's perspective? The only answer I have come up with is that I am particularly concerned to fit the gospel into a message that is needed. Perhaps I have heard one too many preachers go on and on about faith without allowing it to speak to the context in which a congregation finds itself.

My reticence comes from a belief that an inmate's initial inquiries are his way of tentatively searching for a trust to build on in order to ask the real question at hand. Perhaps I have fear of a dependency relationship in which I, as a chaplain, am supposed to have all the answers.

Built into a person's vulnerability is a tendency to say "yes" to whatever gospel is provided no matter who is giving it. Insecurity in an abnormal setting makes it difficult to find the bed rock of normality upon which one can build a firm foundation. I am tempted as a chaplain to jump to the first, easy answer to avoid the harder ones that are lurking beneath the surface.

The subject-oriented nature of my ministry has its philosophical roots in writers such as Emmanuel Levinas. He would say that even in a concentration camp, guards are the initiators of an agenda to which prisoners have the opportunity to respond in grace and empathy. He and Viktor E. Frankl were imprisoned in Germany during the Second World War. They have cause to speak. Levinas suggests that the radical otherness of the person is what defines the context in which the infinite, distance, and divinity become present.[26] This is something that I continue to strive for.

The centurion answered, ". . . but only speak the word, and my servant will be healed" (Matthew 8:8).

4. The Father of Henri Nouwen's Prodigal Son

I began to understand my role as a chaplain when I read the last chapter of Henri Nouwen's book, The Return of the Prodigal Son.[27] Up to that point, I knew what it was like to be the prodigal son who ran away from the authority of his father. I knew what it was like to be the eldest son, who was regarded as the "good boy who never did anything wrong." I felt that the key to the story had to do with these alter-egos discovering a loving relationship with God the Father, through his Son, Jesus Christ. It was only as I began to identify with the father of the story that I could lay claim to my ministry as a chaplain.

Henri Nouwen suggests that true ministry happens when we as pastors and priests own our identities as fathers and mothers to our parishioners. We are to take an active role in mentoring, parenting, and disciplining those we love as our spiritual brothers and sisters. This model of ministry was invaluable in my growing identity as a chaplain. I gained a new appreciation of authority when I was willing to take the perilous risk of spiritual leadership myself. I had to let go of the ways in which my father was not perfect. I had to embrace the mentors who became spiritual fathers and mothers to me. I had the opportunity to pass on the pastoral care I received to others.

A poignant example of what Henri Nouwen had in mind came one day while I was speaking to Leroy, a young offender in dissociation. During the last year Leroy had become dissatisfied with himself. He had alienated his friends and become increasingly confrontational with staff. I spoke to him about the Christmas season that was fast approaching. I was anticipating spending some family time at home. Leroy looked at me and described how a year ago he had been in the park with his two sons, aged 8 and 10, playing soccer. He told me how much fun that had been. He had just started reconnecting with his children before he came to jail.

Leroy stopped for a moment. He looked at me and said, "Don, I want you to do one thing for me this Christmas."

"What?" I asked.

He said, "I want you to go home and spend as much time with your children as you can. If you do that, I will feel as though I have taken care of my own two sons."

I have never forgotten that conversation. My children were just starting to grow up. Leroy helped me set my priorities straight.

God . . . saved us and called us with a holy calling (2 Timothy 1:8-9).

5. Eros and Agape

Several years ago, one of my supervisors told me, "The only thing that chaplains care about is themselves." This person made the remark as a result of criticisms I made about the way chaplaincy was being managed. I went home and had to think about the merits of that statement. Was I thinking primarily of myself in my critique of the system?

I had to admit that I was concerned about the lack of material and social benefits I was receiving as a result of the contract system. It appeared to me to be inherently unjust. I also realized that I had come across as resentful and self-serving. The length of tenure in which this system has been in place contributed to my negative attitude. I had to re-think the nature of my calling, along with the comfort level of my own involvement in ministry.

A book that helped me during this time spoke about the relevance of selfish and selfless love. Anders Nygren, in his book, Eros and Agape,[28] argues in a typically Lutheran fashion that human beings are oriented primarily toward themselves. The goal of their faith is to repent of their sinfulness. As Psalm 14:1-3, quoted in Romans 3:10, iterates, "There is no one who is righteous, not even one." The selflessness of Jesus' *agape* love is in radical contrast to the way human beings treat each other.

Gene Outka, in his book, Agape: An Ethical Analysis,[29] disagrees. While he acknowledges that we are sinful creatures who have fallen short of the glory of God, Outka suggests that salvation is possible because of the spark of goodness that is within us. God created us and the world as inherently good. It is possible to be restored to an original state of goodness through the sacrificial love of Christ as expressed through his willingness to die for others. God became human so that humans could become gods as Athanasius would say.

We should not get hooked psychologically into Paul's anguishing paradox of justification and sanctification that is so evident in Romans 7:21-23. We can live sanctified lives even as we acknowledge the tainted ways in which deeds are done. As I say so many times to offenders, they have to love and care for themselves in order to be liberated to love others. To speak of the dictum in reverse, it is only as we love our spouses more than ourselves that we become supremely self-satisfied. *Agape* and *Eros* are connected dynamically, rather than being in a mutually exclusive relationship. This way of seeing things helped me understand my own motivations for ministry.

For the whole law is summed up in a single commandment, "You shall love your neighbour as yourself" (Galatians 5:14).

6. Taking Charge of the Chapel

Chaplaincy is an area in which things can easily slip away and get out of hand. This is what happened to a new chaplain who was trying to juggle inmates' demands, volunteer commitments, and institutional safeguards. Some volunteers were establishing individual relationships with offenders while attending Sunday evening worship services. This situation grew to a point where offenders were coming to the chapel for the sole purpose of meeting with a particular volunteer. This issue became critical when an offender applied for a "private family visit" with one of the volunteers. Unsure of what to do, the chaplain went to the regional chaplain to ask for advice. The regional chaplain informed him that he should "take charge of the chapel." With this advice in hand, the chaplain banned all the volunteers from the Sunday evening chapel services. He started over with a small group of believers who were committed to their faith and worship.

The sad aspect of this situation was that the chaplain could not deal individually with either the inmates who were coming to the chapel for surreptitious reasons or with the volunteers who had forgotten the purpose of their commitment. It was easier for him to ban all volunteers by hiding behind a rule rather than speaking candidly with the persons who were abusing the system. This approach created ill feelings. The original issue of relationship boundaries was left unaddressed.

I believe that the problem could have been solved if the chaplain would have been brave enough to confront the individuals involved. He chose instead to wait until the situation got out of hand. He then used a "big stick" to solve the problem. This latter solution was effective from an administrative standpoint. It did nothing, however, to bring understanding to the people who were establishing relationships or closure to those who were hurt by this process.

The relationship between our authority and our pastoral role is a complex one. There are times when we as chaplains have to use our authority to ban offenders from the chapel, charge them for breach of rules, suspend volunteer privileges, and establish new rules of conduct to address current and potential risks. There are other times when chaplains are able to intervene personally and pastorally in such a way that the problem is "nipped in the bud." Most importantly, chaplains have to face their own comfort level of power: when to use it and when to not.

You know that the rulers of the Gentiles lord it over them... It will not be so among you (Matthew 20:25-26).

7. How Prison Ministry is Like Getting Married

I was attracted to Naomi, my wife, because of the many ways in which she was different from me. While I was flighty, she was solid. While I was gregarious, she was reserved. While I affirmed my individuality, she was community minded.

Prison ministry can be compared to this example of opposites being attracted to each other. While prison is punitive, I see myself as offering God's redemption. While prison is negative, I see myself as a very positive person. When prison reveals brokenness, I see myself offering healing. While prison life is like looking down a long tunnel with no visible light at the end, I see myself as embodying hope.

Life looks different the longer one is married. Things that first attracted me to Naomi became the very things that I started to resent: being solid meant being traditional, being reserved meant being boring, being community minded meant stifling creativity.

Prison work involved a similiar transformation. While I first saw myself as offering redemption, I began to act more and more like a disciplining officer. After an offender had met me and we had spent an hour talking, he asked me, "Don, aren't you supposed to be more pastoral?" While I first saw myself as offering reconciliation, I found myself recommending divorce and separation in ninety-percent of the cases. While I first saw myself as offering hope, I now preached acquiescence and submission. I began to see myself in a "good cop, bad cop" role. I assuaged inmates' consciences in order to send them back for more discipline and discipleship. My role as a chaplain was to provide enough reality therapy for the inmates to admit, own up to, and pay for what they had done.

Naomi and I have been married for many years. Resentment over differences and irritation at dichotomies have strengthened our relationship. Compromise, forgiveness, regret, acceptance and letting go have helped us move past obstacles to become whole persons. We have become richer by owning the shadow side of our personalities.

I trust that prison ministry can have the same effects. I have realized that the supervising officer may be more merciful than I when it comes to dealing with a situation. I realize that offenders may offer me more hope than I to them. There is a mutual dynamic in which I am part of the larger whole. God is working in spite of, as well as because of, my ministry. God is working through many different people, churches, and organizations.

For salvation is nearer to us now than when we became believers (Romans 13:11).

8. *Lax Security to Make a Point*

Offenders who were transferred to the minimum-security prison at which I worked soon found out that there were lax security measures. A cursory security check was done when they went to the visiting and correspondence area to meet with their families, wives, and friends. These offenders could not wait to get back to their units and tell others about this situation. Soon phones were ringing. Offenders were telling their visitors on the outside that it would be easy for them to bring contraband items such as drugs into the institution.

This situation went on for awhile. One day, just as everything had been arranged for the visitor to bring some drugs in, security stepped in and searched the visitor and offender. They found the drugs, and arrested the two people.

Lax security had been arranged beforehand to see which offenders would be tempted to abuse the system. Inmates who took advantage of the situation found themselves on a bus back to the medium and maximum-security institutions from which they had come. Internal authority was not something they had learned to listen to very well. External authority was still very much needed in their cases.

These incidents made me take notice that security officers were quite familiar with the psychological makeup of offenders. These officers knew what was needed to keep the prison free of drugs. A large picture of a man with binoculars looking directly at the viewer hung in one of the preventive security offices. Staff took their job seriously.

This incident reminded me to clean up my own house. It is easy to let things slide until some inappropriate behaviour puts a damper on our ministry. We become reactive instead of pro-active and end up "playing catch-up." It is much more appropriate to be ready for all situations that may arise. God wants us to make space in our hearts and in our lives and in our sanctuaries so that we are ready to receive God.

Therefore, since we are justified by faith, we have peace with God through our Lord Jesus Christ, through whom we have obtained access to this grace in which we stand (Romans 5:1-2).

9. *Telling Offenders Apart from the Staff*

One of the first things I learned when I transferred to a different prison was that all offenders had the same first name: "inmate." I realized that there were two dynamics at work. First, it was important for staff to know when I called the unit that I was asking for an offender rather than a correctional officer. It was important for operational purposes to distinguish between an inmate and a guard. Staff persons are known as "officers." This helps to keep the lines of authority and rank clear.

The Service has recently re-issued uniforms with the rank clearly marked on the shoulder lapel in the form of stripes (1, 2, 3, or 4). These smart-looking uniforms emphasize the professional nature of the service as well as immediately indicate the role of the person in the prison.

The relevance of these stripes was made clear to me shortly after I started working as a chaplain. On the evening in question, I went directly to the chapel. I started the worship service without checking with the correctional supervisor's office about what was happening in the institution. After the end of the service, a staff member came walking to the chapel area. He made some inquiries. I did not take much notice because I was in the middle of an interview with an offender. On my way out, I walked past the correctional supervisor's office without thinking. The supervisor came out of his office and placed four fingers repeatedly on his shoulder lapel. He indicated in sign language instead of a French I did not understand that he was the manager of the whole institution. I realized I had not paid him the due respect of informing him of what was happening in the chapel. I realized that respect is an important thing to learn when working in a prison environment.

It may not be the Christian names by which we know each other, but the respect and honour we give to each other that makes the difference in our walk of faith. It is, after all, the divine in each person that we are speaking about when we want to know what it means to fear, honour, praise, worship, respect, glorify, love, forgive, and obey.

It is a fearful thing to fall into the hands of the living God (Hebrews 10:31).

10. The Longing for "Virtual Prisons" as a Safety Factor

There is currently a trend in the United States that is pushing for "virtual reality" prisons. These prisons make it possible to have very little physical and social contact between prisoners and staff. Advocates of this system believe that the safety of staff is increased as a result of this approach.

Interestingly enough, inmates and staff at maximum-security prisons already have adopted such an approach to each other. Inmates assume that any fellow resident seen talking to "the man" is an informant who is giving compromising information about other inmates. Conversely, staff who take a personal interest in offenders are seen by their peers as "inmate-lovers." Both of these attitudes reinforce an "us-them" attitude that bolsters suspicion and mistrust of each other.

Part of this mistrust is built into the prison itself. Guards are protected on the inmate living units by glass bubbles within which they work. They give passes, order instructions, and communicate with offenders through narrow window slots. Inmates reinforce suspicion by beating up anyone that is seen talking to a guard. Mutual scorn and disrespect are fostered by both sides.

A lower medium-security prison installed an "open console" system. Communication among guards and offenders occurred on either side of an open platform behind which staff worked. The institution reasoned that this form of personal interaction was more effective than a "closed bubble system." It built trust and respect on both sides of the dividing line. The open atmosphere contributed to a neutral space in which both sides could speak civilly to each other without raising the suspicion of their fellow members. Both sides had to learn to communicate, give reasons for their decisions, and accept responsibility for their mistakes.

I believe that this "open console" system, which has been in place for the past twenty years, has contributed to a safer institution. Offenders and staff realize that positive social interactions can occur within a prison setting where suspicion, mistrust, lack of respect, punishment, and denigration of character are an everyday occurrence.

My dwelling place shall be with them; and I will be their God, and they shall be my people (Ezekiel 37:27).

11. Dynamic Versus Static Security

There has been much discussion about the relative effectiveness of dynamic and static security. Dynamic security has to do with the personal interactions of guards and inmates as they live and work together. Static security has to do with external physical restraints such as fences, locked doors, loaded guns, handcuffs, and cameras. Some prison staff would argue that static security is more effective because it keeps prisoners "out of harm's way." It sends a clear message to inmates about punishment. Others would say that dynamic interaction is more effective because it teaches inmates to respect authority. It teaches officers to communicate with offenders who can be quite difficult.

I would suggest that static security is necessary and effective in the short term. However, it does not address the issue of human care that offenders have to come to terms with if they are going to change. Offenders sometimes have little feeling or understanding of the hurt they have caused others. Inmates sometimes feel that they are the victims and that society owes them for the amount of misfortune and grief they have suffered. Some inmates are more in tune with their own litany of needs and desires than the feelings of others. Static security can cause resentment because it restricts life and limb without exposing the cause and source of this punishment. Dynamic security assumes the need to communicate with real people.

Communication is important because over eighty percent of the inmates will eventually be released into the community. I believe that it is better to learn to speak effectively with them now rather than wait until after they have been locked up in static conditions for many years. Resentment, suspicion, bitterness, and desire for revenge can fester if left unchecked behind closed doors. It is better to get to know the person one is receiving into the community than to guess at his or her intentions.

If then there is any encouragement in Christ, any consolation from love, any sharing in the Spirit, any compassion and sympathy, make my joy complete (Philippians 2:1-2).

12. *The Limits of Personalism*

One of the assumptions that regional and local prison administrators sometimes make is that chaplains can get along with everyone. Chaplains are trained to be personable, diplomatic, lovable, caring, humane, considerate, and trustworthy. They should be able to solve any problem placed before them. This could be a disgruntled inmate standing in the office doorway, an assistant warden who has some problems with chaplaincy, a fellow staff person who considers chaplains too soft and gullible, or a team member who is difficult to work with. All the chaplain has to do is turn on his or her quotient of "personability" and solve the problem at hand.

This personalistic approach can be traced to the I and Thou philosophy of Martin Buber, the theology of John MacMurray, and the Boston school of the 1930s.[30] They believed that a personal relationship between believers and God set the tone for human interactions. All one had to do was to nurture this personal relationship between human beings and everything would turn out right.

Unfortunately, everything does not turn out right if the inmate standing in your doorway disagrees with your decision. Resentment grows if your supervisor micromanages you because of his suspicion of your work. One gets tired of a co-worker refusing to help you pull his or her share of the load. It is difficult to listen to another staff person who dislikes all chaplains as a result of a bad experience.

Personalism in these instances will not "cut it." Something else is needed to rectify a bad situation. Security may have to be called to deal with a disgruntled inmate. The warden may have to be approached to intervene in the situation with your supervisor. A regional chaplain may have to be asked to speak to your colleague. A prayer may be all that one can offer in relation to a disaffected guard. An objective, external force may be needed in some situations that are only tangentially related to a personal relationship with Jesus. Sometimes, the limits of personalism dissolve into the necessities of justice.

See, I am setting my plumb line in the midst of my people Israel (Amos 7:8).

13. *The Catholic Principle of Subsidiarity*

The Catholic principle of subsidiarity states that all decisions should be made at the lowest possible level before proceeding to the next rank of authority.[31] This means that if I have a problem with a particular person or policy, I should first go to that person to discuss the problem before going above his or her head to get satisfaction. I have found this to be an effective approach in prison ministry. Isolating the issue at its most basic level has helped me solve a lot of problems without having to resort to a higher power. Let me give you an example.

One morning in the "hole," I heard the news that an inmate named Justin had received a black eye as a result of an altercation with staff. In spite of staff's reluctance, I was allowed to interview Justin to see what had happened. He told me that he had flooded his cell and wing by blocking the drain to his sink. After he refused to stop when given a direct order, the staff entered his cell and a physical altercation ensued. The prisoner slipped on the wet floor and one of the staff member's boots caught him in the eye as he was going down.

Needless to say, this was a serious altercation that had to be reported to the unit manager. As I stood outside this man's cell talking to him through a four inch by ten inch slot in his door, we could laugh about what had happened. Justin admitted that he was responsible for the altercation that had ensued. There was some inadvertent justification for his black eye.

The same thing happened when I went back to the staff office to speak about the incident. The officer looked at me with trepidation, thinking that I would report him as well as "give him hell." We were able to speak candidly about the incident in a way that put neither of us on the defensive. We, too, were able to laugh about the incident while realizing that the outcome might have turned out worse. The officer could have faced assault charges for what he had done as well as a long investigation. This situation was able to be resolved in a relatively amicable manner that satisfied both parties. I learned that the Catholic principle of subsidiarity was alive and well and could be used to good effect.

If another member of the church sins against you, go and point out the fault when the two of you are alone . . . But if you are not listened to, take one or two others along with you (Matthew 18:15-16).

14. A Military Operation

My job as a chaplain became a lot easier when I realized that the federal prison system is run like a military operation. There is a chain of command from the commissioner in Ottawa to the deputy commissioner in the Region to the warden in the institution to the assistant warden of intervention to the chaplaincy department. Commissioners' Directives, the Corrections and Conditional Release Act, the Mission Statement of the Correctional Service of Canada, Standard Operating Procedures, and Institutional Standing Orders all play a part in the way that rules and orders are implemented. This method of operation helped me understand that a collegial approach is not the first priority. The purpose of a meeting with our institutional supervisor was for him to relay information and instructions to us. It was not our place to question policy or discuss alternative scenarios. When we submitted a proposal, we had to be prepared to be turned down. There were many issues beyond the immediate purview of chaplaincy which administration had to take into account in considering particular requests.

These lines of authority can result in chaplains having to defend some decisions by administration which they personally do not agree with. Chaplains have to become politically astute in order to have some initiatives adopted. They have to become aware of the dynamics of the institution in order to ensure the success of chaplaincy programs.

Chaplains soon learn that the independence of ministry that they enjoyed in their parishes is taken with a grain of salt within institutional life. Prisoners and staff alike are circumscribed by a set of visible fences as well as by a set of spoken and unspoken rules. Religious authority is seen from this perspective as just one more "appeal" that offenders have recourse to in their journey toward healing and hope. Like other sources of authority, ministry needs to be exercised with care and love and justice in order not to be abused and misused.

For rulers are not a terror to good conduct, but to bad (Romans 13:3).

15. The Monster in "Monster's Ball"

I have included a reflection on the movie, *Monster's Ball,* because it illustrates so powerfully the destructive effects of prison on staff. It is not a pretty movie to watch. I would caution anyone who would like to see it.

The movie presents three generations of guards who have worked in the same prison. The movie opens with the father showing his son how to act maturely and responsibly in bringing a condemned man to the death chamber. He shows his son how to strap the man into the chair, and how to watch him die as the chemical injection pervades his body. The problem is that the son is not able to fulfill his duties when the time comes. Humiliated by this process, the father comes home and rails against his son. The son goes upstairs, gets a gun, comes downstairs and shoots himself in front of his father and grandfather.

This tragedy is the start of a long journey of redemption for the father. He is caught between guilt over the death of his son and the arrogance of his own dad. He starts by confronting the racism of his father. He establishes a relationship with the wife of the condemned man. He ends up burning his guard's uniform in order to start a new life as an owner of a gasoline station. One of the final scenes shows the father moving his father to a senior citizens' home while he and his wife rejuvenate the family home.

This movie is difficult to watch because it is so close to the reality of prison work. Staff and inmates are pulled into a morass of mixed-up relationships, morbid reflections, and negative attitudes. Punishment and recriminations are the norm in a world that is anything but normal. The movie suggests that the only way out of this black hole is to leave prison work altogether. There is no redemption within the prison system.

This situation raises the larger theological question about whether punishment is the last word. There are at least a hundred times in the Old and New Testaments when God is prepared to wipe everyone off the face of the earth. The idolatry, wickedness, and self-aggrandizement of the people of Israel made God wonder whether human beings were worth it. Prison staff wonder the same thing. Day after day, they fulfill society's role of punishing offenders by keeping them locked up. When can the redemption of inmates and staff begin?

I lift up my eyes to the hills –
From where will my help come?
My help comes from the Lord,
who made heaven and earth (Psalm 121:1-2).

16. *What Would Jesus Do?*

John Allen, a biographer of Pope Benedict XVI, tells the story of a young ordinand speaking about his first Mass to the bishop. "I had just finished consecrating the holy sacrament. People were lining up to receive communion. I noticed a couple that was not Catholic. As they got closer to the front of the line, I in desperation asked, 'What would Jesus do in this situation?'" "You didn't!" replied the bishop in horror and astonishment.[32]

This little tale shows how the Catholic Church can poke fun at itself for preventing "separated brothers and sisters" from receiving communion during Mass. The rules of the church point toward an objective reality of orthodoxy to which the priests are to adhere.

The priest's invocation of Jesus demonstrates the manner in which the gospel relativizes our most precious concerns. Given Jesus' history of including outsiders, the bishop understood that Jesus might give communion during an occasion when the bishop would not.

There are some rules in the institution to which I adhere in spite of the fact that I may not agree with them. Rules are necessary for the orderly running of an institution. In spite of the fact that they may appear silly or inconsequential from my perspective, they have often been instituted as the result of an incident that caused harm.

The many incidents that occur in prison mean that rules pile up on each other and start overlapping. It can get to a point where a rule becomes applicable in almost every situation. One sometimes feels that there is little room left to breathe.

Administrations and organizations undergo a restructuring process when the weight of the system becomes too cumbersome. A change of commissioner or directives or mission statement is mandated to effect change. This sounds eerily similar to the state of affairs in the Christian church. One has only to look at the development of doctrine, the taboos regarding the blessing and distribution of the Eucharist, and the multiplicity and duplicity of denominations in proclaiming the same gospel to realize that reform is needed everywhere. May Jesus continue to stand in those places where we can not.

Sir, let it alone for one more year, until I dig around it
and put manure on it. If it bears fruit next year, well and good;
but if not, you can cut it down (Luke 13:8-9).

- Chapter Four -

Therapeutic Models of Ministry

1. Removing Obstacles to Achieve Victory

The premise of Bruno Bettelheim's book, The Uses of Enchantment, is that reading fairy tales helps a child face obstacles in his or her life. Fairy tales assume that "severe difficulties are an intrinsic part of human existence." Fairy tales know that "the source of much that goes wrong in life is due to our very own natures – the propensity of human beings to act aggressively, asocially, selfishly, and out of anger and anxiety."[33] These realities are presented in the form of wicked witches, terrifying dragons, and angry step-mothers.

Fairy tales present a hero or heroine who emerges victorious through courageous struggles and steadfast effort against these difficulties. Hansel and Gretel scheme to overcome the wicked witch who wants to eat them for supper. Snow White learns to overcome temptations that the wicked witch presents to her at the house of the seven dwarfs. The third little Pig becomes mature as he outwits the sly hungry wolf.

Fairy tales offer a magical solution to the dilemmas at hand. In the story of "The Queen Bee," the friendly ants, ducks, and bees help Simpleton achieve seemingly impossible tasks. A fairy godmother comes to the rescue of Cinderella in her wish to go to the ball. Snow White is brought back to life by a saviour prince who rescues her from her deep sleep.

These themes are intrinsic to the lives of inmates. They know that they have ended up in jail because of their evil deeds. They will have to work hard to beat what feels like insurmountable odds to be released into society. Inmates have to believe in something beyond themselves to make the necessary changes that will help them become better persons.

As a chaplain, I offer Jesus Christ as a Saviour for the men. I believe that God can help these men come to terms with the deep internal wounds and hurts that they have faced and inflicted on others. Christ becomes the light to inmates' souls as he shows them their dark patterns of bullying, harassment, intimidation, and violation of other human beings. Fairy tales are useful in this regard because they do not shy away from the harsh realities that inmates know so well. Fairy tales, like the Bible, are infinitely optimistic in their belief in the possibilities of transformation.

But during the night an angel of the Lord opened the prison doors, brought them out, and said, "Go, stand in the temple and tell the people the whole message about this life" (Acts 5:19-20).

2. Keeping the Genie in the Bottle

One of the first stories that Bruno Bettelheim tells in The Uses of Enchantment is about a fisherman and a genie.[34] After casting his net into the sea, the fisherman catches a copper jar on the fourth try. He opens it. A giant genie appears and threatens to kill him. The fisherman is able to save himself by asking the genie how such a big person can fit into such a small jar. To prove to the fisherman that he can do anything, the genie stuffs himself into the container. The fisherman quickly re-caps the bottle.

This story is contrary to the usual set of events where a genie grants his liberator three wishes because he is so happy to be set free. The genie in this story has turned gratitude into hatred because it has taken so long for someone to come and rescue him. His long incarceration has made the genie so bitter and angry that he is prepared to kill the first person who sets him free.

How similar to the offenders with whom I work. They have bottled up their feelings for so long that they sometimes explode the moment they are released. What should be gratitude for the person's freedom turns into such a knotted mass of bitterness and rage that the person becomes unpredictable. It is much better in that instance to put the genie back into the bottle rather than risking harm.

Prison is an oppressive and dangerous environment where inmates have to repress their emotions in order to survive. Any demonstration of weakness can result in another offender taking advantage of the situation. Inmates who are released from this situation find it difficult to gauge safe boundaries within which to express themselves appropriately. They err on the side of caution by stuffing their emotions away so that no one knows how they are coping. They err on the side of reckless abandon because, for the first time, they can do things that they were deprived of while inside. Ex-offenders find it difficult to steer a safe course between these two extremes.

It is natural to be confused by the basic errors in judgment that a released offender makes. Most of us do not know what this ex-offender has had to go through for the last three, ten or twenty years in prison. It looks as though the released inmate has no depth perception by which to gauge how fast the car is approaching him. Relationships with the opposite sex can quickly escalate out of hand. A person is tempted to fall back into drugs in order to cope.

Like a roaring lion your adversary the devil prowls around, looking for someone to devour (1 Peter 5:8).

3. *Thousand and One Nights of Healing*

The book, Stories from The Thousand and One Nights, is about a king whose wife is unfaithful to him.[35] He becomes so angry at her betrayal that he has her killed. He then marries a new wife and kills her after their wedding night so that she cannot betray him. This pattern of marrying and killing his new wives on the day after their wedding continues until a woman marries him and tells him a story to delay his action. The tale is so enthralling that the king postpones her killing until she has finished the story. She makes up more and more stories. A thousand and one days later, the king repents of his feelings of anger and revenge toward women. They live happily ever after.

There are valuable lessons to be learned from this simple, if gruesome, tale. Offenders tend to act out in similar ways to which they themselves have been harmed. Molesters of children have often been abused themselves. Offenders commit acts of revenge because they think that this will serve as a means of liberation. The king felt that he could get satisfaction by murdering his next brides. The woman storyteller realized that only an act of bravery, cunning, and sacrifice would cure the king of his hurt. She had to tell an endless number of healing stories for the king to come to terms with his first wife's betrayal. This insight rings true for a prison chaplain. Healing can occur only after the offender has been willing repeatedly to work out the terms of his hurt and understand the offending pattern.

Lloyd was an inmate who was sent back to jail five times because he engaged in the same criminal behaviour within three or four months of being in the community. Every time he was suspended from parole, I would bring out the well-worn drawing of Lloyd's feelings and behaviours that we had outlined at the beginning of our sessions. Lloyd had a "saviour figure mentality" in which he would rescue others in distress. When he could not live up to his own expectations, he would flee the situation and turn to drugs. It was only after Lloyd began to accept himself for who he was, instead of who he wanted everyone else to think he was that some progress was made.

I learned from this experience that it takes at least a thousand and one nights of healing in order for the king to forgive his wife. The new bride, who stands in for his first deceptive wife, has to repeat her acts of love again and again so that the king finally realizes that not all women are like his first wife. He slowly moves from "his awful imaginings" to true love.

The heart of her husband trusts in her, and he will have no lack of gain (Proverbs 31:11).

4. The Usefulness of Fairy Tales

I remember the night I was reading The Cat in the Hat Comes Back[36] to one of my children. I came to the startling realization that this was less of an innocent tale than I had imagined. On the surface, Dr. Seuss was speaking about how letters of the alphabet can be shaped into words so that big messes can be cleaned up. He was also speaking about the coming of age of two adolescent children, about marriages and progeny, and about how salvation can come in the midst of the stain that life makes. I had no idea how relevant the works of the psychologist Sigmund Freud and the sociologists Emile Durkheim and Max Weber were to this seemingly innocuous fairy tale.

This story had grownup meaning for me because I deal constantly with infantile desires within adult men. In spite of the surface rationality that is manifest, we have non-rational needs and emotions that are hard to name. Most of the men with whom I work have never put these feelings into words. They have acted out on their unconscious emotions for which they have received long sentences. It is only after the fact that they realize the anger, rage, and emotional needs that they have. For some, it feels as though it is too late to start over. Their recognition of the pain they have caused comes only after their harm of others has been devastating.

Dr. Seuss is able to articulate the important things of life in simple terms. He illustrates how an old man can still have joy even though he is dying. He conjures up the imagination of a lad who lives in the midst of an infinitely boring routine. Dr. Seuss makes a peasant boy with stilts fall into friendship with a grumpy king in a castle. He describes the letter "Z" as a mysterious "Voom" that can clean up snow. Judith and Neil Morgan, Ted Geisel's biographers, demonstrate how these plain insights came after thirty years of hard work and mediocre results. It was not until Ted Geisel was asked to build a story on the basis of two hundred and twenty-five words that The Cat in the Hat came alive.[37] The most harrowing and narrowing of circumstances can bring out the best in people. One has only to think of George Washington Carver and his discovery of the usefulness of peanuts to realize how much can come from so little.

The jar of meal will not be emptied and the jug of oil will not fail until the day that the Lord sends rain on the earth (I Kings 17:14).

5. *On Beyond Zebra*

One of the more interesting commentaries on the Enlightenment and its emphasis on rationality comes from a little book by Dr. Seuss entitled, On Beyond Zebra.[38] Two small boys are standing in front of a blackboard at school. They are trying to outdo each other in drawing letters of the alphabet. Finally, one of the boys draws a large elaborate letter with loops and swirls. He tells the other boy, named Conrad Cornelius O'Donald O'Dell, "Knowing the letters A to Z is nothing. Let me show you what happens when I make letters that go beyond Zebra." The rest of the book includes a lexicon of new letters with fancy calligraphy and made-up names that refer to things that are not included in the alphabet.

Dr. Seuss is illustrating the fact that life can not be totally explained by the use of language. One has to go beyond the alphabet in order to express what one is feeling. This inexpressibility is referred to as "Voom" in The Cat in the Hat Comes Back.[39] The non-rational part of life is symbolized with elaborate figures and nonsensical names in On Beyond Zebra. One quickly gets the idea that one has to go beyond the alphabet in order to communicate.

Inmates identify with this story because they also have gone beyond the As, Bs, and Cs of societal norms to express their rage, revenge, anger, selfish desires, and lack of control. Their impulsiveness, lack of discipline, and need for wanton destruction have exceeded the bounds of decency. These acts can be referred to in sociopathic terms because they go beyond the realm of rationality from a common point of view.

Dr. Seuss is helpful because he understands that these behaviours and actions need a lexicon of their own in order to find a reference point within reality. The psychological and social sciences' discovery of the unconscious has gone a long way in making these non-rationalities comprehensible. They have provided signposts beyond ordinary language to humanize the inhumane and demonic. These liminal flashpoints enable offenders to find a language to communicate the reasons for their behaviour. It also helps them find a pathway towards hope.

May we know what this new teaching is that you are presenting? It sounds rather strange to us, so we would like to know what it means (Acts 17:19).

6. Coming to Terms with Unconscious Desires

Psychologist Sigmund Freud and sociologist Emile Durkheim understood the power of the subconscious.[40] The "id" has the ability to ignore the reprimanding "superego" as well as refuse the "ego's" demands to channel its energies in appropriate ways. Offenders regress to infantile behaviour when faced with daunting situations and fearful repercussions.

This point was driven home when I started working with Anthony. He wanted to speak about offences for which he had not been convicted. Anthony felt the chaplain's office was a safe place to "come clean" about the criminal activities in which he had been involved.

Our work together became a cathartic experience. Anthony realized the extent to which he had been, and still was involved in criminal preoccupations. A great burden was lifted as we spent two hours together each week speaking about things which until that point had remained unspoken. Anthony was able to accept, admit, and own the many devious activities in which he had been involved.

I was not sensitive to the fact that Anthony was becoming more and more agitated during the course of our sessions. He realized that the more he shared, the more time he could be facing as a result of his confessions. I had made the limits of confidentiality clear, was monitoring his behaviour and asked him each week how he was coping. It was not, however, until he acted out in a particularly inappropriate way that I realized that the strain had become too much. By that time, it was too late. Anthony was placed into segregation for six months and eventually moved to a higher security prison. Anthony had made some progress by coming to terms with his identity, offending patterns, and things he was doing to change.

Anthony was like a chameleon that could hide his feelings behind his acting out behaviour. His acting out was a way of letting me know that he could not deal with the realities with which we were coming face-to-face in my office. Anthony had to bail out of the situation.

I should have taken more time to make sure that Anthony's current behaviours matched his ability to cope with the "can of worms" that was opened up as he began to share intimately about himself. We had no idea where it would lead.

If we confess our sins, he who is faithful and just will forgive us our sins and cleanse us from all unrighteousness (1 John 1:9).

7. Integration of a Dual Personality

The reason it takes so long for some offenders to get caught is that they get an immense pleasure in living a double life-style. While a person is a wonderful parent during the day, he is a molesting grandfather at night. Although he is a successful contractor in the community, he is also the head of a criminal gang that extorts money from businesses. Although he is a competent professional to his clients, he is an abusive partner in the marriage relationship. These double life-styles can go on for a long time. Offenders gain a sense of power in hiding behind these two aspects of their personalities.

There is a point when the schizophrenic reality of this split personality becomes untenable. A man who straddles a boat and dock eventually falls into the water when the boat drifts too far away. Often, an offender feels relief in "coming clean" about who he really is. Falling into the water is more comforting than living with a split personality.

A lot of air is released when the balloon bursts. The sharing that takes place is often so profound that a chaplain is unprepared for the record of events that are being described. For the first time since childhood, the offender feels free enough to share about a shameful part of his life that has been left unspoken. Some lived in survival mode as a result of a neglectful mother. Others became distrustful because of a parent's abuse. Violence of care was simply passed on in other cases. In most situations, there was an experience so fundamental that the offender was willing to rape, molest, hurt, rob, and even kill others in order to get his revenge for "what happened to him."

The offender's deep feeling of resentment makes him willing to take almost any action to see that "justice" is done. Simultaneous relief and anguish come when the offender realizes that he has now hurt someone as much, if not more, than he himself has been hurt. The fact that he was raped by his mother makes the offender understand why he has gone on to molest so many other people.

There is no guarantee that an integration of a dual personality can take place. Dr. Jekyll goes insane when he realizes what he, as Mr. Hyde, has done.[41] What is needed is help - from God and others - with these dual personalities.

They . . . saw the demoniac sitting there, clothed and in his right mind (Mark 5:15).

8. *Focusing on One Cure in Order to Offend in Another Way*

One can spend so much time focusing on one thing that one ends up losing out in other ways. This happened to at least two offenders with whom I worked. One of them came to see me about an offence he had committed. Matthew was deeply remorseful for what he had done and worked conscientiously in his program to address his issues. I was able to help him with an autobiography that he was asked to write to understand his crime cycle better. Over the course of a year, Matthew came to understand that abandonment, isolation, transience, and lack of emotional bonding had all contributed to his disregard for others. His callous attitude toward himself spilled over into his willingness to hurt others.

By the time of his release, I was confident that Matthew had enough insight into his life to reintegrate into society. He was committed to settling down instead of moving from place to place. Matthew built on the support of family, friends, and volunteers. I encouraged him to keep in touch with me about how he was doing.

About six months later, I received a call from a distraught volunteer who was a community support for Matthew. The person informed me that Matthew had fallen in love with a volunteer's wife. This caused a marriage break-up. The volunteer asked me to get in touch with Matthew and convince him to break off his relationship.

One of the things that surprised me when I spoke to Matthew was that he saw nothing wrong with what he was doing. He explained to me that the former marriage had been "on the rocks." This was why he and his new girlfriend were living together. He was merely being of service by helping the wife of the volunteer find true love.

Matthew had no idea how right he was. He recognized the neediness of this woman and exploited her vulnerability for his own ends. Matthew had gained insight into his first offence, which was criminal. He had not yet learned to be empathetic toward another person's fears, hurts, and desires. Matthew had become convinced from an early age that life revolved around himself. Everything was looked at from the point of view of what Matthew could gain from the situation. He was not able to respect the boundaries of marriage that the volunteer couple brought into the circle. Now other family members were suffering because of Matthew's actions.

How is it that you have contrived this deed in your heart? You did not lie to us but to God (Acts 5:4).

9. The Significance of Near-Death Experiences

The meaning of death came up as a topic during a Bible study. As each person shared around the circle, I realized that everyone except me had had a near-death experience. Many of the men had been in car crashes. Some of them had had drug overdoses. Others had tried to commit suicide. Still others had been stabbed.

These experiences were in keeping with the high-risk adventures in which these men had given themselves permission to be involved. They were willing to test the limits of life – and death. The lives that had been theirs as young children involved so much violence, drugs, and abandonment that they seemed to care little whether they lived or died. Their high-speed cop chases delivered a huge adrenaline rush. It was similar to what their middle-class peers on the right side of the law experienced when they skied down mountain slopes.

I probed deeper into the reasons for such behaviour. These scenarios escalated every time these men faced serious emotional turmoil. "Acting out" for some followed immediately upon the death of their father or mother. A spree of criminal activity occurred in other cases when a final link to their step-parents or siblings was severed. In almost every case, someone had given up caring for the offender. In a manic cry for help, the offender put himself in a high-risk situation to draw attention to his plight. These men had ceased caring for themselves and everyone else. They were willing to "die by cop" or take one too many concoction of drugs.

This is a dangerous moment of reckoning. Once a person has ceased loving himself, he does not care how many people he takes with him to fulfill his death wish. Misery loves company. The internalized suffering and pain are vented onto as many people as it takes for others to understand what an individual is going through. Hope and love have been replaced by a black hole.

The sharing that was offered around the Bible study table that night was a moving experience. I will never forget the heart-felt emotions that were spilled as each person shared what they had been through and the reasons for their actions. The psalmist seems to understand where they were coming from.

But I am a worm, and not human; scorned by others, and despised by the people (Psalm 22:6).

10. Hidden Signs of Redemption in The Woodsman

The Woodsman is a powerful movie about a sex offender who is released into the community. The person works hard at changing his life until he slowly starts slipping back into his old habits and devious thoughts. The climax of the story is so disturbing that one of the persons with whom I was watching the movie had to leave because he could not stand to see what would happen next. The story is ultimately redeeming as the viewer discovers more and more about the man.

I encourage offenders to watch the movie in pairs. I ask them to talk with me or another person after they have finished viewing the movie. There are so many different aspects to the movie that it is interesting to hear what insight each viewer gained. One participant shared how judgmental the police and psychologist were of the man. I begged to differ. I pointed out how the policeman, with his gruff exterior and condemning attitude, found a place in his heart to believe in the ex-offender's ability to change. This act of caring was exemplified in his third or fourth visit. The policeman moves a plant on the kitchen table so that it will receive more light. This insignificant gesture demonstrated to me that the policeman was able to be redemptive, even if it was done hesitantly and with a great deal of apprehension.

The reason I noticed this act of courage was because I work with so many staff that have become thoroughly jaded by their work. They see offenders returning again and again to prison with new convictions. This perception is exaggerated by the fact that we as prison staff see only the offenders who come back to prison. The ones who have gone on to become law-abiding citizens are invisible. The little act of grace on the policeman's part spoke volumes to me because so many of his co-workers would scoff at even the thought of reaching out in kindness. Staff have been disappointed so many times by offenders. Some decide that the best policy is to believe in no one at all (not even in God). It is because of this prison reality that the small act of moving a plant was so significant for me in the movie.

If you do good to those who do good to you, what credit is that to you? For even sinners do the same (Luke 6:33).

11. *Three Dimensionality in a One-Dimensional World*

One of the handicaps in interviewing an offender is that the chaplain is being presented with only one side of the story. It is hard to get a three-dimensional picture of what happened. The victim is not there. The family is not there. The police are not there. The community is not there. The chaplain has to fill in the red, green, and orange colours to augment the grey and blue background that is being presented.

A memorable example of this phenomenon happened to me as I was working with a Croatian offender by the name of Yasha. Yasha spoke very poor English and French. He tried repeatedly to make me understand the anxieties he was having. In spite of my best efforts, weeks went by without me getting a clear picture of his fears. Yasha made clear to me that he had killed his wife. He was of a particular faith group and was struggling with some unresolved issues. Neither a member of his faith community nor volunteers that spoke his language were available to assist him. We struggled on together, trying to communicate.

I was finally able to speak to a distant relative about Yasha's anxieties. I learned that he had killed not only his wife, but also his son. I learned that Yasha had signed some papers about a year ago allowing the sale of his house to pay for lawyer's fees. This relative had been present at the signing of these papers. She was able to reassure Yasha that the monies were being handled in a responsible manner.

I have learned to be attentive to what is not being said. I have to listen to the background noise from which a three-dimensional reality can emerge. I am reminded of Edgar, an older man who spoke only about his wife and his former work. It was as though the rest of his life did not exist. I learned later that he had offended against his grandchildren. I knew then why Edgar never spoke of his children. I am sorry that I did not push him a little further in this direction. I should have asked him how his offences against his grandchildren had affected his family.

By wisdom a house is built, and by understanding it is established (Proverbs 24:3).

12. Death and Birth

The irony of a hospital is that in the midst of sick and dying people, pregnant mothers are having babies. In the midst of aging patients, sophisticated equipment, and vociferous diseases comes the cry of a new baby. We feel confident enough of our medical facilities to allow our babies to be nourished there until they and their mothers are healthy enough to go home.

What a theological statement! God felt safe enough about the world to have God's Son born here. God sent his Son so believers could understand what it is like to have trust and confidence and faith in a new birth. Innocence occurred within the context of betrayal, sacrifice, suffering and death. Innocence was reborn in the fashion of a resurrection. A second naïveté is possible only after the mask of childhood has been stripped away. The adulthood of wrongful intentions needs regeneration. Jesus goes about healing the sick and raising the dead. Redemptive suffering enables old ravished bodies to become youthful and idyllic again.

Prisons are crucibles of the gospel. The tiniest baby steps of faith occur within emotionally insecure men who are trying to come to grips with the harm they have caused. Innocence is reborn within the crucifixions that are realities in their daily lives.

A larger question has to do with the extent to which we let the medical metaphors of disease and contamination rule our view of crime and punishment.[42] The social sciences believe that crime is a forensic matter that can be excised through the scalpel use of behaviour modification, rational re-programming, and association re-direction. Human beings are rational matter that can be healed through the intravenous drip of "angers and emotions management," the pill of phallymetric testing, and the physiotherapy of thinking tool retention.

I work with offenders whose parents have just died. Their girlfriends have just left them. Their sisters have been killed. Their crimes are difficult to admit, much less confess. Their drug use is persistent. They have come back to prison umpteen times. Life appears to go beyond the ability of human beings to cope. There is something essentially non-rational that has to be owned in order for the rational to emerge. That something is deeply spiritual.

I came that they may have life, and have it abundantly (John 10:10).

- Chapter Five -

Programming Aspects of Chaplaincy

1. Setting a Direction for Ministry

I developed a spiritual journey curriculum to set a direction for ministry. The seven sessions involved 1) letting go of obstacles, 2) reflecting on one's family of origin, 3) being mentored by others, 4) finding a spiritual centre, 5) becoming involved in the world, 6) letting the Spirit work, and 7) acknowledging the mystery of life.

The inmates found this journey to be helpful. Many of them had been abandoned by their families and parented by their peers. They were living without any real sense of where life was going. These young men ended up in jail before they realized the full impact of their crimes.

I created a portable labyrinth to set parameters for these seven sessions. I suggested that we have to take three steps inward, one step in repose, and three steps outward to arrive at our destination. The first three steps involved letting go of our attachments, letting go of our co-dependent relationships, and moving beyond our spiritual mentors. We had to recognize our woundedness so that we could replace this pain with something more positive. I suggested that this center, the fourth step, was Jesus Christ.

Our movement forward can begin as we build on the faith that we have found. Taking time to centre ourselves has the paradoxical effect of enlivening us for ministry. We become inspired to help others because we no longer have to worry about ourselves. Liberation of the Spirit makes us unafraid of where the chips may fall. The mystery of life is something we can fall into without being fearful that we will get lost.

This spiritual journey represents a refreshing path on which hesitant believers and curious seekers can travel. Many inmates with whom I work are afraid to come to the chapel because of the stigma of religion. Others are so steeped in their criminality that they have no time for anyone but themselves. I have been challenged to find ways to work with these men. The spiritual journey course is one small way that I have reached out.

Long ago God spoke to our ancestors in many and various ways by the prophets (Hebrews 1:1).

2. *Water Running Downhill*

When we were small, we would dam up the little streams of water that flowed in the ditches along country roads. We would spend hours diking up the channels with mud and clay. We would stand back and watch how long it would take for the running water to overflow its manmade banks.

This image helps me understand how God is working in prison. God will find a way to the ocean no matter how long it takes to get around the obstacles that human beings have set in God's path. All we have to do is allow ourselves to float as a piece of driftwood on this meandering waterway. God will find a way to release us from the bonds in which we are entangled. The purposes of God are finding their way downhill through the force of gravity.

I invent ever-new ways of getting offenders' attention. One day, it may be the use of a labyrinth. The next day, it may be a Young Adult Group. The next year, it may be a Christopher Leadership Course. The year after that, it may be a choir or a worship band.

I care more about reaching the men than the means to get their attention. Each situation provides a new set of circumstances for which one needs to be attentive. Each obstacle to ministry has to be recognized for what it is: a built-up wall of clay and mud that is causing the flow of water to move in another direction. We have to allow ourselves to be led along this counter-intuitive route until such time as God allows the walls to come down. If we believe that God's purposes are flowing downhill, we do not have to worry about how long it will take to get there.

"God is working his purposes out as year succeeds to year,
God is working his purposes out, and the time is drawing near;
Nearer and nearer draws the time, The time shall surely be,
When the earth shall be filled with the glory of God
As the waters cover the sea."[43]

As soon as the people heard the sound of the trumpets, they raised a great shout, and the wall fell down flat (Joshua 6:20).

3. *The Accuracy of the Human Sciences*

Over two hundred young offenders resided at one of the federal institutions in which I started working. These men, aged eighteen to twenty-five, were considered at risk to re-offend because they had little respect for themselves or others. They had very little support from their families. They were prone to mouth-off against staff and other inmates at the slightest provocation. They travelled together in small groups in the prison.

Some of these men caused a disturbance in the yard one Saturday afternoon. They threw eggs at some family members and jeered at participants in a baseball game. As a result of this incident, I began a "Young Adult Group." We discussed topics such as respect for authority, impulsiveness, peer pressure, crime cycle, job skills, relationships and resources. I facilitated this group as a course, gave certificates for graduation, and submitted evaluations on their behalf to their parole officers.

Randy and Jeremy were two offenders who were leaders among their peers. They were motivated to share and committed to change. They led by example. They shared personal experiences and reflected on the reasons they started doing crime. They set career objectives. I appreciated these offenders' input. I submitted positive evaluations of their progress.

These evaluations were in keeping with the statistical data of the number of offenders who would not re-offend. The behavioural sciences verified that six of the eight offenders would not commit another crime during the next two to four years. The human sciences could not tell me *which* of these offenders would remain crime free. That evaluation was left up to the individual judgment of the facilitator.

I was usually wrong about who was making progress. Randy and Jeremy were actually further into their institutionalization and crime cycle than I (or they) realized. Randy ended up being transferred to a maximum-security facility while Jeremy continued to deal drugs on the street. They were so good at being natural leaders that they scarcely missed a beat. They could convince almost anyone of anything.

The offenders who were trying to change were either too ashamed to share what they had done, or too fearful that their sharing would not be kept confidential. I learned to listen to these stumbling, awkward responses. Their testimonies were genuine and would fall within the human science prediction of the six that would not re-offend.

Not every one who says to me, "Lord, Lord" will enter the kingdom of heaven, but only the one who does the will of my Father (Matthew 7:21).

4. Surviving by Staying Medicated

The first three topics in my "Young Adult Group" course had to do with authority, family of origin and peer pressure. I suggested to participants that offenders go through a process of criminal association and anti-social behaviour before they become involved in criminal activity. Once these activities become full-blown, the offenders are often caught and sent to jail. Inmates are then faced with a crucial decision in their lives. Do they really care about themselves? Have they reached the point where they have given up on themselves and are willing to act out violently again?

I suggested that inmates have two options in regard to their crime cycle. If they no longer care about themselves, they will isolate themselves and continue in the criminal life-style to which they are accustomed. If they do care for themselves, they will find pro-social activities in which they can participate. They will work on job skills and establish positive personal relationships.

Offenders responded to my input by saying that there was a third option available. One of the best ways of getting through this situation was to stay medicated. Using drugs was an excellent means of dulling the pain of incarceration, assuaging the guilt and shame of one's crime, and getting through the night of broken relationships.

This was one option that I had not considered. It was such an obvious one. This choice was available at almost any street corner and in a number of places in the institution. Inmates had learned to survive very well on their own with a little help from a mood-altering substance. The easiest way to jettison one's emotional and social baggage was to "do a line of cocaine." This kept a person going for at least another week, if not for another year. "Who cared what happened after that?"

This third option made me realize the extent to which it is difficult for us to deal with our problems. We find different ways to avoid the situation. Offenders see staying medicated as a realistic option for them to survive. The question that I ask is this: "Is there not more to life than surviving?"

Simon answered, "Pray for me to the Lord, that nothing of what you have said may happen to me" (Acts 8:24).

5. *Going Backwards to Understand the Future*

An offender by the name of Gerald recounted how a gun had miraculously appeared in his hand. He had accidentally fired it, luckily not causing life-threatening injuries. It was true that the gun was not his. A friend had supplied it. I questioned Gerald as to what the gun was doing there in the first place.

There were at least ten factors that led up to the crime. First, the two families involved did not get along with each other. Second, animosity between the offender and victim was evident during some sporting events in which they were both involved. Third, this situation escalated when the offender made a threatening phone call to the victim. Fourth, friends sided with one or the other protagonist. Fifth, both parties consumed alcohol to fortify their resolve. Sixth, the offender as well as his friends felt it prudent to bring along some weapons in case they were needed. Seventh, the friends assumed that the other persons were also bringing some weapons along. Eighth, they met at a location where there was enough fear of a possible attack that a gun was given to Gerald. Ninth, Gerald felt it necessary to take the offensive because of his fear of being assaulted. Tenth, Gerald felt comfortable enough with having a gun in his hand that he used it.

I am always amazed that the situation is presented as occurring spontaneously. It is as if combustible materials suddenly caught on fire. Some years ago, a television station aired a series about a hotel. It portrayed various characters having to solve ethical dilemmas. One woman felt she had to sell her body in order to buy medicine for her child. A priest felt attracted enough to a woman that he rented a hotel room to see whether he wanted to continue the relationship. The viewer was only introduced to the scene when the choices appeared limited and the results inevitable. He or she was not allowed to back up the time line. The viewer was not allowed to ask how these characters got themselves into these ridiculous situations in the first place. People give themselves permission to get involved in boundary situations.

For which of you, intending to build a tower, does not first sit down and estimate the cost, to see whether he has enough to complete it? (Luke 14:28)

6. Leaving One's Tools Behind

The most frequent response I hear when inmates have been suspended from parole is: "I left my tools behind." These tools represent the rational coping skills that they learned to use while in prison. These implements abandoned them in a moment of crisis. They are like the carpenter who left his hammer behind and tried to solve the problem with an axe. Ex-offenders revert to their most familiar patterns of behaviour when "push comes to shove."

There are two main reasons for these lapses of judgment. The first is that offenders are not always rational human beings when faced with a dilemma. In spite of the fact that they have learned to cope relatively well in prison, these social skills leave them in a moment of crisis. Drug use or violent retaliation is the default means by which ex-offenders have learned to cope.

The second reason for these lapses of judgment has to do with the controlled environment of a prison. Offenders are often in the best condition that they have ever been while in jail. Jack had been sober for three years after twenty years of life on the street. He understood the nature of his crimes. He made his first contact with one of seven children whom he had abandoned seventeen years before. He had a spouse waiting for him when he was released. The miracle is that Jack has now been in the community for five years since I last saw him.

Others are not so lucky. George reverted within a few hours of being released to doing drugs with Jane, his girlfriend. He had agreed in the drug rehabilitation program never to see her again. He agreed with the facilitator that Jane represented a high-risk factor. The ecstasy of doing drugs with her when he was released, however, more than made up for the four years in which George was incarcerated. Unfortunately, this euphoria only lasted until George sobered up inside the remand centre.

I sometimes think that sentencing offenders "to the street" would be the best way for them to learn to become law-abiding citizens. Inmates experience the most suffering and pain and inadequacy when they have to deal with real life jobs, relationships, and bills. There should be a controlled environment available in which they can learn to live in the community. This could be their greatest "punishment" as well as their greatest learning experience. We all need to know what it means to live life more abundantly.

Brother Saul, the Lord Jesus, who appeared to you on your way here, has sent me so that you may regain your sight and be filled with the Holy Spirit (Acts 9:17).

7. Step One of Alcoholics Anonymous

I work as a liaison officer for the Alcoholics Anonymous group in prison. I help the group find volunteers to come into the institution as well as assist them in organizing social gatherings. A.A. members ask me to help them work through steps four and five of the twelve step process

I remember Frank, a young president of the group. During a conversation, I asked him at what stage he was in the A.A. program. He told me that he had not yet accepted step one. That step involved admitting that one "was powerless over alcohol and that one needed help." Being president of the A.A. group was a status symbol and position of power for Frank. It did not matter to him where he was in the twelve step process.

This conversation reminded me of another one that I had over twenty years ago. Rudy, a fifty-five year old man, went to prison a number of years before I was born. He had been to prison four times and was doing a four-year sentence when I met him. I remember asking Rudy if he was an alcoholic. "Oh no," he said. "I am just a binge drinker." I asked Rudy when he got into trouble. "Oh, during my week-long binges. Other than that, I am fine. I am a hard worker."

This conversation demonstrated to me how difficult it is for us to face our short-comings. Rudy clutched his status as a hard worker close to his chest while meandering in and out of prison for the next forty years as a result of his drinking habits. Rudy would "rather die with his boots on" than admit he had a problem with alcohol.

The effectiveness of the Alcoholics Anonymous program is in the humility it dishes out in good doses. Gloria, a woman volunteer at one of the Round-ups, shared how she had lived with alcohol for twenty years before admitting it was a problem. She would go from one fantasy life to another dream world rather than admit she needed help with her relationships, career, life-style, and friends. It was only in the last ten years that Gloria had been able to accept herself as she was. She challenged the guys to "think realistically." Gloria spoke about how she was content to live in a small apartment. She was satisfied to work at a relatively low, but comfortable wage. She found fulfillment in the job that she was in. She maintained healthy relationships with people who accepted her and were loyal to her. None of these small achievements had been possible during the twenty years that Gloria had been hiding behind a bottle. I was touched and moved by her simple testimony.

For while we were still weak . . . Christ died for the ungodly (Romans 5:6).

8. An Empty Box

Jerry was being disruptive in an "employment readiness" course. He would make sure that everyone was as distracted as possible. When this game became boring, Jerry would sulk in the back of the room. He would ask to take as many bathroom breaks as possible. He would put his feet up on the desk. This situation was made worse by the fact that Paul, the facilitator, could not kick Jerry out of class. Jerry had been mandated to take this course by his parole officer.

The course finally came to an end. Paul arranged certificates for every member of the class, including Jerry. When Jerry's turn came to receive his award, Paul motioned him to the front. "Jerry, I have decided to give you a gift as well as a certificate. You may open it in front of the class." With a smirk on his face along with a question mark, Jerry opened the box. It was empty.

This story haunts me. While the teacher's gesture could be viewed as facetious, it sent a clear message to Jerry. He had contributed nothing to the class. In fact, he had made it difficult for everyone else to concentrate. Paul was simply returning the favour.

I meet people like Jerry every day. They have a knack for making things worse. In spite of my attention and care for them, they find endless ways to make anything serious into a joke. One person hid in a chapel washroom and trashed an office. Another person stole candles and altar cloths from the chapel until we had a security officer check his cell and retrieve the items. The person did not care that he had been caught. Everything was a game to him.

I am not sure what can be done for people like Jerry. There is so much woundedness inside. Beneath the veiled frivolity is a viciousness that has no bounds. Harm, ridicule, hurt, and punishment is the only thing people like Jerry have learned to do to someone who gets close to them.

Say to wisdom, "You are my sister, and call insight your intimate friend (Proverbs 7:4).

9. Concord Place

Concord Place was a half-way home located in the country for inmates on parole. They went there for three months as they made the transition from prison to the community. Clive, the director, operated a farm with cows and horses that the ex-offenders took care of. The discipline of a regular work routine along with the earned wages helped the men get established.

I received mixed reviews from the inmates who were sent back to prison from this half-way house. Some suggested that Clive was too strict a disciplinarian. Others found the farm work unrelated to their job interests in the city. I took these remarks with a grain of salt. These statements were coming from men who had been suspended from parole.

Several volunteers and offenders requested that I invite Clive to come and speak at the chapel. An opportunity came in the form of a job fair being held in the gymnasium. Different community groups set up displays and explained their role in the reintegration process.

I met Clive at the fair and introduced him to the warden. Clive explained that this was the first time since the late 1960s that he had been in this institution. At that time, he had been a boxer and had gotten into trouble with the law. After serving several years, he had been released. He had started this half-way house as a way of helping others become law-abiding citizens.

The warden, volunteers, and inmates expressed their appreciation for Clive's work. They were impressed with the way Clive handled himself. He had recently received a college degree for counselling troubled youths. He had found a way of integrating work experience with the emotional and social challenges that these young men faced.

Within a month of this presentation, the front page news reported that Clive had been picked up for a concealed weapon, drug trafficking, and uttering death threats. The report went on to note that Clive's two sons had been in trouble with a local gang. Clive had felt it necessary to get involved. Clive reverted to the lessons he had learned on the streets in his earlier life. The thought of his sons being killed was too much for Clive to handle. He took the law into his own hands.

This scenario has repeated itself countless times during the course of my ministry. Police officers, parole officers, chaplains, volunteers, newspaper reporters, and churches have all been caught in the trap of giving someone who is not ready the opportunity to give a testimony.

You will know them by their fruits (Matthew 7:16).

10. Community Service for Minimum-Security Offenders

The Royal Canadian Mounted Police did not feel comfortable in allowing minimum-security inmates to do community service in our county. A series of meetings were held to discuss the matter. After some deliberation, the RCMP agreed to accept this project on a trial basis.

The assistant warden, unit manager, and three parole officers identified ten inmates they felt would be suitable to be supervised in the community. A meeting was convened at the local RCMP office to go over the names and offences of the eligible candidates.

I was thrilled about this possibility. The local arena needed to be painted. A wilderness camp needed maintenance work done. The golf course managers were always short of help. The history museum needed "sprucing up."

My sense of satisfaction dissipated as I sat in that meeting and heard the offences of these eligible inmates read out. In that moment, I, as "Joe Public," wanted to stand up and shout, "No! Look at the horrible things these men have done. They are going to be a risk to me and my family. Keep them locked up." All the security officers and policemen were nodding their heads in grave agreement to let these men work in our community. There was irony in that moment.

Only two men have walked away since that program was started over ten years ago. They were re-captured within the week. Hundreds of men and thousands of work-hours have been devoted to making the community a better place to live. The men are paid $5 a day for their efforts. Each night they return to the minimum facility where they will have to remain for another one to three years.

While grateful for the assistance, the community has been unsure of how to show their gratitude. I sometimes feel that there might be a public outcry if more people knew that supervised inmates were doing community service. Unintended consequences are an unfortunate reality of working in the prison system. Please pray for this community service from which inmates derive a lot of satisfaction in giving something back.

Godliness is valuable in every way, holding promise for both the present life and the life to come (1Timothy 4:8).

- Chapter Six -

The Role of Volunteers

1. Knowing Who You are Before You Start

Gloria, a volunteer who came with her church to the prison chapel services, was a little shy. It took her a while to get used to the prison setting as well as the offenders who attended the chapel services. After some training and further involvement, Gloria began to feel more comfortable with her ministry.

I took no further notice of the situation until one day George approached me and mentioned that he had noticed that Gloria was single. I did not make comments about the situation. It was noticeable that George found Gloria easy to talk to. Sometime later, George was released into the community. He began attending the same church that had been involved with prison ministry. He participated in several Bible studies and eventually got up the courage to ask Gloria out for a date.

I first heard about the situation when David, the church volunteer coordinator, phoned me and told me that Gloria no longer wanted to be involved in prison ministry. Although Dave gave me no details, I had already heard from George that Gloria had rejected his advances.

Gloria realized something in this encounter. She had begun volunteering to see if she would be attracted to someone in prison. George could sense this ambiguity and desire within her. That was the reason he got up the courage to ask her out for a date. It was only when George brought this mixed message into the open that Gloria understood that she was not open to a relationship with an ex-offender. Although she quit prison ministry, George helped her gain a more realistic and open understanding of what she was seeking in life.

The sad ending to this story is that George continued to be rejected at a variety of levels by friends and family. The last straw came when his brother-in-law refused to let George see his sister in the hospital. George gave up his apartment, started using drugs again, and was soon back in prison for a lengthy sentence. George had not yet learned to deal with his feelings of bitterness and alienation at the rejection that he had come to know so well throughout his life.

> *But strive for the greater gifts. And I will show you a still more excellent way (I Corinthians 12:31).*

2. *Making Promises a Person Can't Keep*

A tattle-tale sign that an inmate is in trouble is when he starts making promises he cannot keep. I remember Henry, an offender in Dissociation and Segregation, who was going to be released into the community. I asked him how he was doing. Henry told me that he was going to get a job. He was never going to use drugs again. He was never going to "frequent" downtown again. He was not going to go back to his old friends. He was not going to go back to his family. He was going to start going to church. He was going to "make up" with Cindy, his girlfriend. Henry was going to start attending Bible studies.

Half-way through the conversation, I realized that Henry was very scared of being released. He had no idea what he was going to do. He would probably go back to using drugs within the first few hours of being in the community. No one in the world had cared for him except Cindy -- and she had "dumped" him. I was present when Cindy had refused Henry's advances. It would take much more than the faith of a mustard seed for Henry to get on the right path. Henry had spoken to me about his violent crime and about the problems he had with his father. I knew that Henry was confused. He was facing many emotional, spiritual, social and identity challenges when he was released.

I was very much like Henry when I first became a chapel volunteer. I told John that I would show up at his parole hearing. I told Bill that I would bring in a special Bible. I told Nathan that I would contact his wife and ask her why she was not coming to visit. I told Sergio that I would call his Embassy and ask them about the status of his immigration hearing. I came back a month later and had not done any of these things. The look on the offenders' faces told me that I had made promises I could not keep. I realized that doing all of these helpful things is not what the inmates were really asking for. They wanted someone to accept them for who they were. They wanted someone to listen to the challenges they were facing. They wanted someone to help them be realistic in their expectations of themselves as well as of me.

If you abide in me, and my words abide in you, ask for whatever you wish, and it will be done for you (John 15:7).

3. *Wiccan, Gay, and Criminal*

The challenge of being a volunteer in prison was brought home to me one night. I was in the company of Ed and Rachel, a Christian couple. They were visiting Tim, a young offender, as part of a friendship program. I knew Ed and Rachel through church connections. I had also worked with Tim. As we spoke about the Christian faith that the couple and I shared, I wondered how comfortable Tim felt about sharing his life. I knew that he condoned and was perhaps involved in a gay lifestyle. I knew that Tim was attracted to the more questionable practices of Wicca. I was aware of the disturbing, almost predatory nature of Tim's crime. It had caused a lot of fear and anxiety in the community. Which of these aspects of his life would Tim be willing to share with Ed and Rachel? To what extent could their friendship handle this sharing of information?

Ed and Rachel had faced significant challenges in their family and church life. They provided community support to ex-offenders. They were under no illusions about what these men were all about. And yet, as I sat there, I had to ask myself about the degree of acceptance that was demanded by their faith. Were Ed and Rachel really able to accept these aspects of Tim's life? Did Tim sense their willingness to listen as an invitation to share about things that were clearly out of the realm of their Christian experience? There is a difference between the evangelical motivation of one's calling and the ability to listen in a non-judgmental manner.

It is always amazing to me that the most evangelical Christians, the most orthodox Catholics, and the most conservative Jews feel called to prison ministry. There is a huge disconnect between these believers' world views and those of the offenders. Why should I have doubts about the love of God? Does God not give us the ability to understand Tim's situation more fully? It has sometimes taken over two years for an offender to share his personal journey with me. We can all be touched by the healing balm that the gospel offers.

I pray that you may have the power to comprehend . . . the breadth and length and height and depth, and to know the love of Christ (Ephesians 3:18-19).

4. A Volunteer Help Line

Samantha went on a radio talk show to recruit new volunteers for a program entitled Circles of Support and Accountability. Between four and seven volunteers form a circle and establish rapport with a core member, who is an ex-offender. Samantha spoke about the mutual support that volunteers received from each other. She spoke about the sense of satisfaction that volunteers and core members felt as they ministered to each other. After a brief discussion with the host of the program, the phone lines were opened to see if there were any people listening who would like to help.

The listeners' responses caught Samantha off-guard. "Yes," all the callers responded, "I would love to be part of the program. I need help too. Setting up a circle of support for me would be greatly appreciated." The responses were similar to the Monty Python skit about a "suicide help line." They were asking for something different from what was intended. The *CoSA* program sounded so promising that Samantha now had a whole new set of referrals to deal with.

I can identify with Samantha. The most frequent inquiries I get after a church presentation about prison ministry are from victims who have been afraid to talk to anyone about their abuse. Some people would like to volunteer because of the deep wounds they themselves have experienced.

There was something so inviting about Samantha's words that radio listeners wanted to receive the same kind of care and attention. She made them feel safe enough to call and tell her that they also needed help. We all need a place of safety to discuss things which are too personal to share. There is something wonderfully anonymous about public talk shows that people feel led to share some of their personal struggles.

I have been moved by the willingness of volunteers to share some very personal experiences. It was often this time of sharing that helped them understand why they were attracted to prison ministry. They now had to decide whether they wanted to continue.

To those who are called,... May mercy, peace and love be yours in abundance (Jude 1-2).

5. Someone Else Should Do It.

About six years ago, several volunteers set up a support group for high-risk sex offenders. Between four and seven volunteers met with these core members each week to help them get re-established. A contract was set up in which the core member agreed to abide by his release conditions. The circle of volunteers agreed to meet with the core member on a regular basis.

Thirteen Circles of Support and Accountability have since been set up in that city. The Circles work closely with the High Risk Unit of the City Police as well as the forensic unit of the hospital. These organizations provide training for the program. The volunteers are drawn from a variety of walks of life. There has been a dramatic reduction of risk in each of the cases. The core members have found a sense of belonging within this volunteer family. They have learned pro-social ways of coping with life.

The group was asked to establish *CoSAs* in another city as a result of the success of this program. The director interviewed candidates for the coordinator position. She met with the police to ascertain the need for this program. She consulted with psychologists to see if they could provide training. In spite of the goodwill expressed by all concerned, no one felt led to head up the program. Some candidates did not know where to find volunteers. Others found the salary to be nominal. Still others felt that working with these high risk individuals was too time-consuming and risky.

I asked my colleagues what we should do. One of them said, "Someone else should take the responsibility in monitoring these high-risk offenders." How right he was! Someone else should be responsible for making sure these men do not offend again. The trouble is that no one wants to get involved. Police cannot be a 24/7 monitoring service. The forensic unit is only available during office hours and in emergencies. "Joe Public" has no idea of the issues some lonely man on the street corner is facing. Isolation is often the highest risk factor. Emotional bonding between the core member and volunteers enables a pro-social community to be established. The sense of belonging that is created diffuses the more glaring fear factors that are an integral part of these offenders' histories. These men have become the pariahs of our society with whom almost everyone is afraid to work. This is a challenge for our communities. How will we respond?

The crowd sternly ordered them to be quiet; but they shouted even more loudly (Matthew 20:31).

6. The Role of Volunteers

There were some problems with volunteers when I started working at a new institution. Sometimes they were turned away at the gate because they did not have proper identification. Sometimes their names had been inadvertently left off of an approved memo. At other times the security officer had suspicions about what the volunteers were bringing into the institution.

The volunteer coordinator and I established a variety of measures to deal with these problems. We conducted a day-long training session. Officers spoke to volunteers about the "dos and don'ts" of the institution. We were able to get the volunteer clearances increased from one to two years. The assistant warden helped us access a data base on our computers. We could check which volunteers were cleared for a planned event.

There continued to be miscommunication and incidents. I finally went to an administrator's office and told him about the problem. During the course of the conversation, the administrator told me, "The volunteers are a lot of work for our staff. They are at risk when they come into the institution. I wish we could establish a committee that would ban all volunteers from prison." I stood there for a moment, speechless. Finally, I said, tongue-in-cheek, "That's great to know. Could I be in charge of that committee?"

This conversation helped the administrator and I to get on the same page. We could agree that volunteers are a disruption to the routine of the prison. They represent a certain amount of risk because they have not been trained in the same way as staff. They are in some ways naïve.

At the same time, the administrator was able to see that volunteers represented a needed relief from the boredom and negative atmosphere of the prison. Inmates who were engaged in volunteer programs did not have time to get into trouble on their units or cause a fight in the yard. Volunteers provided hope in ways that regular staff could not. Through his candid admission and our concerted joint efforts, the administrator and I were able to come to some mutual agreement.

And the king will answer them, "Truly, I tell you, just as you did it to one of the least of these who are members of my family, you did it to me" (Matthew 25:40).

7. When Two Hundred Meters is Further than Two Hundred Kilometres

Once a month, volunteers drive more than one hundred kilometres to visit prisoners in the institution in which I work. They visit inmates on a one-to-one basis or in a chapel group. The offenders appreciate these efforts. They start preparing on the afternoon of the evening visit. They hope that lockdowns, illness on the part of the volunteer, or some other incident will not interrupt the planned encounter.

Volunteers receive a lot of satisfaction from their visits. They comment on how much they have learned. The inmate shares about a world that is often radically different from that of the volunteer. The listening abilities of the volunteers provide a context for normalized conversations. The inmates grow to depend on these important outside contacts.

The inmate may sometimes not want to visit his sponsor. He may be playing baseball in the yard, attending an Alcoholics Anonymous meeting, or is simply occupied in another venue. A visit by a volunteer can become a fall-back plan in case nothing else is going on.

The volunteer coordinator meets with the inmate when he has missed a visit with his sponsor. They go over the reasons for the lapsed visit. The inmate is usually apologetic and promises to be there the next time. When a pattern of missed visits develops, the inmate is dropped from the group.

There are a number of cases in which an offender starts to isolate himself from the world. A denied parole, breakup of a relationship, or disappointing chapel service may be to blame. A sense of hopelessness begins to invade the inmate's sense of wellbeing. He starts doing a lot of "cell time." He quits his work, drops his friends, and becomes pre-occupied with his unhappy situation. This is a dangerous moment. Suicide can easily become the best solution that the inmate sees for himself. It is times like these when walking two hundred meters from the unit to the chapel or visiting area is a lot further, both physically and mentally, than the two hundred kilometres the volunteer has had to drive to see this person.

Stay awake and pray that you may not come into the time of trial (Matthew 26: 41).

Jesus behind Bars

Opportunities for pastoral care

Black: Each person has a dark side.
Colours: Each Person has many attributes.
Circles: Each person intersects with the other.
White: Each person has a future.

Then the angel showed me the river of the water of life,
bright as crystal, flowing from the throne of God
and of the Lamb (Revelation 22:1).

Inclusiveness of the Symbolic[44]

Distanciation of the Literal[45]

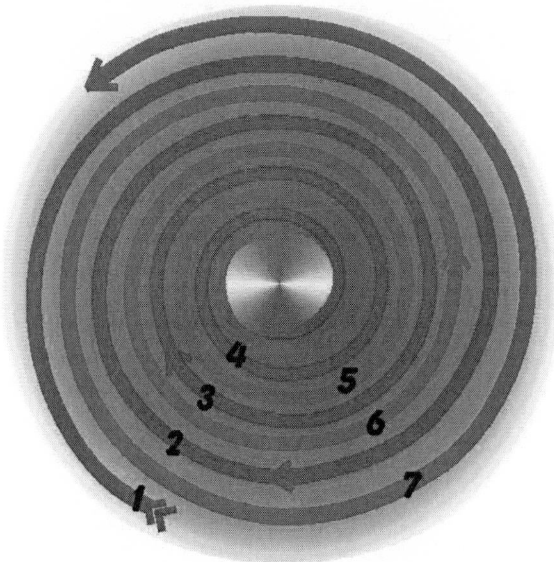

Labyrinth of God

– *PART I I* –

- Chapter Seven -

Challenges of Ecumenism

1. Abjurement Forms and the English Language

One of my tasks as an English Protestant chaplain within a predominantly French Catholic milieu was to solve the ecumenical problems that had arisen during the previous years of ministry. The former French Pentecostal minister had brought a bathtub into the prison and baptized all those who requested it. He proceeded to give all the new converts abjurement forms by which they could renounce their Catholic faith and affirm their new found Christianity (Protestantism).

This action caused quite a bit of consternation on the part of the Catholic priest along with the regional chaplain. The Protestant and Catholic chaplains decided to ask inmates to limit themselves to attending one of the two services provided. Strict attendance was taken by both parties.

By the time I came on the scene, there was a pervasive atmosphere of suspicion of all chaplains. I was carefully scrutinized about my beliefs concerning the Protestant as well as Catholic faiths. After several days of reflection, I came upon the following solution. I would conduct my services in the English language while the Catholic priest would hold his services in French. This resulted in the odd but workable solution of having English Protestants and Italian Catholics attending my services. The French Catholics and Haitian Protestants attended the priest's services. The Spanish Christians were the only group that remained to be figured out. They continued the Pentecostal/Catholic battle that was being waged in their respective South American countries.

The Catholic priest and I learned to trust each other. There were the occasional suspicious glances sideways when a Spanish Protestant ended up in my service. In this way, the kingdom of God was advanced in ways that surprised us all.

I ask . . . on behalf of those who will believe in me through their word, that they may all be one (John 17:20).

2. Are Catholics Christian?

The question of whether Catholics are Christian was poignantly focused for me when I received a call from a French Pentecostal minister. She was wondering if she could get involved in prison ministry at a minimum-security institution where I was "on call." I acknowledged that the Protestant church provided only an occasional visit from a Free Church pastor. She indicated that her interest was primarily with French inmates. She had worked for more than twenty years in another province establishing various churches.

We continued our telephone conversation. I indicated that it was not likely that I or we would start a French ministry at the institution to which she was referring. As she expressed her regrets, she made the following remark, "Is it not sad that there is no one to minister to the more than 200 inmates in that prison?" As I reflected on her remark, I replied, "Well, I know of at least one person who is ministering to them." There was about a half minute of silence on the other end of the line until she realized that I was speaking about the Catholic priest. She replied, "Oh, I see what you mean." That ended our conversation.

This conversation forced me to consider whether I believed the Catholic priest at the institution could lead offenders to Christ. Was that a job that was up to us Protestant Christians? It made me decide whether the Catholic priest and I were fellow brothers in the Lord. Were we trying to establish parallel paths to heaven? Protestant or other types of worship services were perhaps needed in the institution. They, however, should not be offered until there is a clear understanding of their common cause with other Christians ministering at the institution.

One of the favourite Protestant principles is the idea that the "church is constantly reforming itself." I think our Catholic brothers and sisters would agree with that statement. They would point to numerous instances in the last two thousand years when the Catholic Church has responded to various crises with the liberating word of the gospel. The iconoclastic controversy of the fourth century demonstrates how images touch us to the core. Some religious streams are established where images are taboo. Others are created where representations of human beings are an integral part of worship. Let us continue to honour each others' religious roots, traditions, and confessions through which we worship.

On entering the house, they saw the child with Mary his mother, and they knelt down and paid him homage (Matthew 2:11).

3. Ecumenism and the Rope of Inclusivity

Ecumenism is something a chaplain deals with as soon as he or she starts working in prison. Volunteers come from a variety of Christian backgrounds. Chaplains are from various denominations. Chaplains share a common chapel. They accommodate each other in terms of the use of crosses, altars, tabernacles, religious banners, sacramental items, baptismal fonts, basins, coverings, and musical instruments. This ecumenical reality helps one recognize the essentials of one's Christian faith as well as those aspects of one's faith that are not as important.

Ecumenism has its challenges. This became potently evident during a retreat in which Protestant and Catholic volunteers came together for a weekend workshop. Volunteers shared during the Friday and Saturday sessions about their ministry in prison. The facilitator placed the participants in a large circle. He unfurled a long rope that each person passed along as they shared their testimonies of ministry. The rope served as a powerful symbol of community building, solidarity with offenders, unity with each other, and strength of purpose and courage before God. What made the experience even more pregnant with meaning was the fact that this workshop happened within a French and English setting. Historic differences of language compounded religious partialities.

This idyllic retreat came to an abrupt end on Sunday morning. The Catholic priests tried to figure out where they were going to hold Mass. The Anglican priest announced that he was going to hold an English service in another room. The French and English Pentecostals were left to figure out how to conduct a service of their own. In spite of meticulous planning, the organizers had "forgotten" to talk about what was going to happen on Sunday morning. A likely reason was that this issue was too delicate to discuss. Everyone had been left to their own devices.

In the afternoon session that followed, the Catholic volunteers expressed their displeasure at the obvious differences of religious practice that had taken place in the morning. Why could the Protestants not receive communion together with the majority of Catholics that were there? Needless to say, the rope of inclusivity was now stretched and frayed beyond its tested strength. I have always been amazed at how prison ministry draws people together from all walks of faith, in spite of the divided visible body of Christ of which we are a part.

There is one body and one Spirit, just as you were called to the one hope of your calling (Ephesians 4:4).

4. *Veronica and the Stations of the Cross*

One of the non-biblical references in the Stations of the Cross is to the woman Veronica. She is left with an imprint of Jesus on the cloth that she uses to wipe his face. A biblical literalist of the Protestant variety would say that this is an insertion of human imagination into the biblical passion narrative that undermines the usefulness of such a journey for a believer. I might have held such a view in my earlier Bible College days. I have since come to the opposite conclusion. A conjunction of our imagination and the biblical story is necessary for the story to come alive. This is, in fact, what the Catholics had in mind by introducing Veronica into the picture. "Vera-icon" means a true representation of Christ that is "imprinted" from the page into the body to the heart. Representing Christ to the world is accomplished in the "stations of the cross" through the introduction of a woman bystander with whom contemporary believers can identify. She is not a foreign witness who does not belong. Veronica provides the door by which we can enter into the passion of Jesus' life, death, and resurrection.

There are a myriad of ways that the Catholic Church uses to help believers gain access to faith. John the Baptist, Mary, the Eucharist, saints, and icons help to locate Jesus as the Saviour, Lord, Master, and Ruler of this world within the heart of the believer. These tertiary signs originate in secondary effects which have been enacted by the providence of God in which Jesus, the Christ, is the primary figure.

A Mennonite example would be that of a fellow believer who mirrors, embodies, reflects, and exemplifies Jesus in his or her daily life. Is it possible that discipleship, pacifism, sacrifice, humility, *gelassenheit*, self-effacement, bearing one's cross in silence, and turning the other cheek are "icons" by which the Believers' Church presents Christ to the world? Who knows, perhaps a representative of the radical Reformation named Anna Baptist could stand in for Veronica when it is the Mennonites' turn to re-enact the road to Calvary during Easter week.

Consider that the holy woman named Veronica, seeing Jesus so afflicted, and His face bathed in sweat and blood, presented Him with a towel with which He wiped His adorable face, leaving on it the impression of His holy countenance.[46]

5. A Stake instead of a Cross

Iconoclasm takes many forms. Jehovah Witnesses claim that Jesus was crucified on a stake instead of a cross.[47] I was puzzled about the importance of this issue. One day as I was facing the front of the chapel, I realized what these brothers and sisters in Christ were trying to tell me. They were saying that they could not even worship in the same chapel as I did because there was a cross hanging there. The cross was integral to an unreformed and unenlightened established church, of which I, as an Anabaptist, was a part. I must admit, it felt funny to be associated with the established church under whose racks my great-great ancestors suffered. The cross has become the new dividing line between the Christian church and the Kingdom Halls.

I should not be surprised at this turn of events. The Jewish Rabbi has also refused to use any chapel designated for Christian services. Taking the cross down does not make any difference to him. The Muslim Imam has similar reservations in terms of images that are used for religious purposes.

We live in a dominantly Christian culture. We do not realize the extent to which our separated brethren disagree at a fundamental level with our Christian presumptions. This became clear again to me as I was sitting with some colleagues at a luncheon during the High Holiday season. The issue of singing Christmas carols came up. The Jewish psychologist suggested that he could not sing these songs. A fellow colleague innocently asked, "Why not?" "Well, the word 'Christ' is in Christmas," he replied. "This means that I would be confessing Jesus as the Messiah if I sang these songs." "Wow, you are fussy, aren't you?" the unthinking questioner responded. I came away from that conversation with a new appreciation of how much difference there can be between being fuzzy and being fussy.

The Jehovah Witnesses are even fussier than we are about Christmas trees, crosses, the Trinity, and Jehovah. This puts us on notice as to the degree to which we believe in Christ from a certain perspective. From their 16th century perspective, Anabaptists would find it incomprehensible to see the ways that I am being re-inspired by Catholicism. May the cross be a sign of peace, not a cause of division among us!

When they came to the place that is called The Skull, they crucified Jesus there with the criminals, one on his right and one on his left (Luke 23:33).

6. *Red and Yellow, Black and White*

I remember a children's story that a Korean pastor told during a Daily Vacation Bible School class. He explained the creation of the world this way. "God's creation of human beings is like baking bread. He put the first batch into the oven but he took it out too soon. He put the next loaves of bread into the stove but waited too long to take them out. Finally, he put the last batch in and it came out just right."

I recall this story because it made me realize that being "white" is, perhaps, not the ideal solution that God envisioned. The world ended up with a variety of colours of race. It is up to us to decide how to deal with this situation.

A similar "ah hah" experience occurred when some inmates noticed a picture of a white Jesus hanging on one of the walls in the chaplain's office. They suggested that Jesus had the swarthy features of a Mediterranean man. His skin colour was more in keeping with their own than with mine. The picture eventually disappeared.

The multi-coloured nature of faith was driven home in another way. A logo was hanging in front of the multi-cultural centre that the aboriginal inmates used for their gatherings. The colours, red, yellow, black and white occupied the four quadrants of the large circle. In that moment, I recalled the Sunday school song that I had learned at an early age:

Red and yellow, black and white,
All are precious in his sight.
Jesus loves the little children of the world.

These illustrations raise the question of how successful we as Christians have been in cultural integration. I remember a professor of mine who converted to Christianity in his early twenties. He went to the worship services of different denominations to see which one he wanted to join. He finally chose the Catholic Church because the most ethnic groups were represented in that congregation. This should stand as a lesson for us all. We believe in the inclusivity as well as in the enculturation of the gospel.

. . . There is no longer Greek and Jew, circumcised and uncircumcised, barbarian, Scythian, slave and free; but Christ is all and in all (Colossians 3:11).

7. Pentecostal Exuberance and Catholic Reverence

The British sociologist David Martin suggests that Pentecostalism and Catholicism represent the two options for a global church.[48] The Catholic Church offers a worship experience based on "locality, birthright membership, continuity, and extended familial and communal obligations." By contrast, Pentecostalism finds its *raison-d'être* in "individual choice, movement, fraternal association, and the nuclear family."

I find myself agreeing with David Martin on the basis of my experience of worship in prison. Inmates are attracted to the continuity and order of the Catholic Mass. Confession, forgiveness, prayers, scripture readings, hymns of response, and the Eucharist form an organic whole into which the inmate is worshipfully immersed. The set structure produces a silent ecstasy of the Spirit that moves the inmate beyond the mundane.

A similar experience is offered in the Pentecostal service through a significantly different means. Here, repeated stanzas of praise songs, testimonies of transformation, heartfelt prayers, and dramatically presented sermons form a locus of the new with which the Christian can identify. Thirty men gladly go to the front when asked to show their commitment to the Lord. Individual prayers and a "laying on of hands" commences as the congregation bows its head. An uplifting of the Spirit occurs that is similar to, yet different from the Catholic service. Exuberance and reverence combine to form an organic whole.

My ministry has been drawn into these two polarized options. As soon as the Pentecostal service ends, inmates come and ask me when these volunteers can come again. As soon as the Lutheran lectionary service that I use is over, inmates come and tell me how much they appreciated the service. The Pentecostal service offers spontaneity and freshness. The fixed order of my scripted service represents a familiar experience of the divine. Individually spoken prayers during the prayers of the faithful, Prayer and Praise music in between the readings, and occasional testimonies have enabled me to combine the rational and the irrational. I try to play down the polarization of experience that prisons manufacture. The ordered nature of the high-church liturgy has become a meaningful part of my ministry. At the same time, I remain open to those who experience healing and the leading of the Holy Spirit through other forms of worship.

They devoted themselves to the apostles' teaching and fellowship, to the breaking of bread and the prayers (Acts 2:42).

- Chapter Eight -

Challenges of Inter-Faith Dialogue

1. The Inclusiveness of a Symbol

A logo in the centre of this book features half of a cross, half of a crescent moon, a disassembled Star of David, the outline of a tepee, and a semi-circle of inclusivity. The religious symbols of Christianity, Islam, Judaism, and aboriginal spirituality have been modified in order to find room within the open-ended circle of care that is prison ministry.

Religious symbols are powerful because they incorporate a multiplicity of meanings within them. The cross refers to Jesus' crucifixion, life, and resurrection, as well as more broadly to Christianity. It refers to the horizontal dimension of human interaction and the vertical dimension of divine/human contact. It represents an earthy figure of wood on which God died.

The other symbols are just as powerful. The moon of Islam and star of Judaism point to the God in heaven who looks down on our mortal existence. Our aspirations and expectations are relativized by a God that is bigger than we are. The tepee, in turn, represents a transient existence within a spiritually alive world of nature. Aboriginal peoples understand to a greater extent than Caucasians what it means to be dependent on nature.

I have included different religions within one symbol to show the importance of inter-faith respect in prison chaplaincy. Our ministry is offered within a space in which a variety of religious expressions are cultivated. Room is provided for the Muslims on Friday afternoons, for the Jews on Saturdays, and for the Christians on Sundays. Sweat lodges are situated adjacent to the chapel as a complement and critique.

The dean of a Presbyterian college once took me for a walk. He pointed to the steeple on top of the chapel. He told me, "We felt that it was better to put up a steeple instead of a cross. God is greater than all of our divine names and symbols. A steeple affirms this transcendence and opens up communication with other religions in a way that a cross does not." There is a steeple on top of the prison chapel in which I work. I trust that the inter-religious symbol at the centre of this book invites dialogue across cultures and faiths.

From one ancestor he made all nations to inhabit the whole earth . . . so that they would search for God and perhaps grope for him and find him (Acts 17:26-27).

2. *Distanciation of the Literal*

A second logo at the centre of this book features the distinct religious symbols of Islam, Judaism, Christianity, and aboriginal spirituality set against a Zoroastrian-inspired circle of the sun.

The purpose of this logo is to invite discussion of the differences among religions. The first, inclusive logo invites dialogue and communication. The second, literal image is intended to help us name our religious peculiarities.

Paul Ricoeur has spoken about this process of distanciation.[49] He uses the example of the Bible to make his point. The Bible not only comforts us in its acclamation of salvation. It also distances itself by showing us how far we have fallen from the grace of God. The scenes of war and violence in the Old Testament, the judgmental passages of the New Testament, and the fearful pronouncement of "falling into the hands of a living God" (Hebrews 10:31) make us aware that the text criticizes us as well as includes us.

A similar experience is at work in our encounter with other religions. Sometimes we are struck at how similar various faiths are. This makes us conclude that we worship one God in different ways. At other times, we are confronted by the vast differences among religions. The strict monotheism of Islam and Judaism makes us realize how polytheistic our human Jesus and Trinitarian formula looks from their perspective. We have called a human being God. We Christians fail to realize how audacious that sounds.

The distance that is created by our encounter with other religions is a healthy one. It is precisely the differences that enrich and deepen our understanding of the divine. I am attracted to my wife because of her distinct way of doing things. I am able to understand my personality better in light of her differences.

A similar procedure is at work in a dialogue with other religions. I have become a more devout Christian as a result of my involvement with Jews, Muslims, Wiccans, aboriginals, Zoroastrians, and atheists. I have had to look more deeply into the scriptures to understand why I can confess Jesus Christ as Saviour. May the differences and similarities among us draw us closer to the heart of the divine mystery.

But Esau ran to meet him, and embraced him, and fell on his neck and kissed him, and they wept (Genesis 33:4).

3. Becoming a Good Moravian Disciple

One of the duties of a prison chaplain is to authorize religious diets for offenders who require special meals based on their religious beliefs. Jews require kosher meals, Muslims *halal* food, Hindus vegetarian meals, Rastafarians natural (ital) foods, and Seventh-Day Adventists non-pork products with a preference for vegetarianism.

Chaplains receive many requests for religious diets. Anything different from the standard prison fare is viewed as a privilege for the inmate. Verifying the religious status of each offender can be an onerous task. Some religious communities simply take the word of the offender. Some do not have initiation rites. Others are quite loose in their organizational structure. It can be difficult to get a written letter of authorization, especially when offenders are from other countries. Discretion becomes the rule of thumb in some cases.

One of the offenders I worked with was Richard. He was from Barbados. He had convinced the French Catholic chaplain at the reception centre that he needed a special diet based on his Moravian beliefs. Richard was transferred to the institution where I worked. He came and showed me the religious diet authorization he had received. I laughed and told him that it was unfortunate that I knew something about Moravianism. I knew that Barbados was one of the places where Moravians had a mission. I also knew that Moravians did not require a special diet.

Richard took the response in stride. In fact, we became good friends as a result of the little "gaff" that he had tried to pull on me. Within a few weeks, he was coming to chapel services. He felt included by the volunteers and grew in his Christian faith. Is it not wonderful how a little sore point like the denial of a religious diet can turn into something positive?

See, I am sending you out like sheep into the midst of wolves; so be wise as serpents and innocent as doves (Matthew 10:16).

4. Mennonite Mafia

Almost all cultures and minority peoples have groups within their communities that are involved in gangs. This pertains as much to the Iranian community as the Sri Lankans, the Colombians as well as the Italians, the aboriginal peoples as well as the Chinese, the Iraqis as well as the Russians, the Lebanese as well as the Algerians, the Indians as well as the Sikhs, and the French as well as the English.

Gangs are one way for marginalized peoples to find a place of belonging within society, albeit in an infamous way. Gangs are a common occurrence in new immigrant groups, at least for the first generation. If integration of the ethnic group into society does not take place, gangs continue to be active. The young Islamic minorities within Britain and France, along with some of the aboriginal young people in Canada, are examples of the failure of integration.

One of the surprises I discovered is that gangs are a part of religious minorities as well. There was a point within the social dynamics of Montreal that people were referring to various offenders as belonging to a Jewish Mafia. At about the same time, there were news reports of a Mennonite Mafia exporting marijuana across the Mexican border to Texas.

Some Mennonites felt that the press coverage should not have mentioned the religious status of these offenders. The word "mafia" should not have been associated with this group. I reflected on this affront to sensational news reporting. It is important for us to acknowledge these people as our own. The news reports make us aware of our flaws as a denomination in keeping our ideals of faith and discipleship alive. It makes us aware of our responsibility to the seeds that have fallen on hard ground.

Those who are well have no need of a physician, but those who are sick (Mark 2:17).

5. Rastafarian Connections and Accountability

Rastafarianism is a faith derived from Judeo-Christianity that began in Jamaica in reaction to the ruling colonial British government. Symbols of this home-grown faith include smoking marijuana as a key ritual, growing one's hair into dreadlocks, eating naturalistic foods, and wearing a cap with the green, yellow, and black colours of the Jamaican flag. Smoking marijuana is linked to the mandrakes that Leah sold to Rachel in order to lie with her husband Jacob (Genesis 30:14-24). Wearing dreadlocks is reminiscent of the Nazaritic vow that Samson made to God (Judges 13:5). Vegetarianism is linked to the kosher laws of Leviticus 11. The head covering is a nationalistic response to Britain combined with a vicarious identification with the tribes of Israel (Galatians 4:25, Revelation 1:14-15, 5:5).

One difficulty in working with this group was that they considered me to be part of their problem. First, they were in prison, which was considered an unclean place. Second, I, as a Caucasian, was part of the Babylonic oppression against which they were fighting. I had a tight balancing act to follow. It took me weeks to find a minister who could confirm that these men were Rastafarian. He then refused to see me for the same reason as the offenders. I was unclean. He told me that I would have to take the word of the men with whom I worked.

The next challenge was convincing the kitchen staff that Rastafarianism was a real religion. Those adhering to this faith were entitled to naturalistic foods. We convened a meeting with all parties concerned. The kitchen staff was impressed with the devotedness of the offenders who had made the request.

I encountered another problem. It was reported in Parliament that unknown chaplains were seen handing out marijuana to a group of offenders. I responded to the anxious call from Ottawa by saying that, as far as I knew, marijuana was still an illegal drug. In spite of religious requests, I could not offer any to these men.

One of the positive outcomes that resulted from these challenges is that I had to work closely with this group. My job was to ascertain which person was Rastafarian. The men made sure that newer devotees would attend their Bible study group for at least three months before the person was eligible for a religious diet. After that period of time, I was willing to endorse each of the men's religious practices with a signed form. We learned much about each other's faith and came to respect each other's beliefs.

No razor shall come upon the head; . . . they shall let the locks of the head grow long (Numbers 6:5).

6. Clean and Unclean Practices

The concept of clean and unclean became important when I phoned an Islamic Imam and asked him to come and visit one of the offenders in jail. The Imam told me that he could not come to the prison because it was considered in Islam to be an unclean place. This issue became even more urgent when I asked him if I could give a copy of the Koran to an inmate. When the Imam learned that there was a toilet in every cell, his answer was no. The inmate had to find another place besides his own "house" to read his sacred scriptures.

A similar incident happened when I began to work with aboriginal people in the West. The elders in the community did not want to erect a sweat lodge within the confines of the prison. They were afraid it would become contaminated by the prison's poisonous effects.

How right they were to be afraid! Anyone who steps into the atmosphere of prison life has to be prepared to be "touched by the dastardly deeds" that are committed there. One is reminded of the famous Howard Hughes' movie in which he started washing his hands over and over again. He had a morbid fear of contamination by germs and disease. This fear is at the forefront in our hospitals. Staff infections can wreck havoc on patients who are recovering from successful surgeries and medical procedures. The hospital can become a toxic culprit in addition to being a healing balm.

The imam and the elders had reason to wonder whether so much evil in one place could co-exist with the good. I am happy to report that radical changes for the better can take place in prison precisely because everyone is so aware of what is not working. The reality of illness forces a person to find a way to rise above it. That is why God can be such a powerful force in prison. Prisoners know exactly what needs to be worked on. A lot of prayer and grace and confidence need to be claimed in order to defeat evil.

To be sure, this process of justification and sanctification is messy. The categories of clean and unclean become fuzzy as everyone wrestles in the mud to bring evil under control. Prisoners and staff and wardens and chaplains alike learn to let their "yes" be "yes," their "no" be "no" and to be clear in their expectations, demands, and promises. I can not help but think of Peter's vision in which a great sheet full of reptiles, animals, and birds of the air descended from heaven. God declared them clean (Acts 10:12). I sometimes feel as though I, like Peter, am on the reality television show, "Fear Factor." I am asked to deal with bugs and snakes and wasps in the course of my daily work.

What God has made clean, you must not call profane (Acts 10:15).

7. Rocking the Cradle of Christmas

I had a moving inter-faith experience when I escorted several Tamil offenders to a Hare Krishna temple. These offenders wanted to partake of a Hindu religious festival celebrating the birth of Ram.

The event went well in spite of the fact that the guru of the temple had some questions about who I was. There were heaps of vegetarian food, scripture readings, a meditation, some dancing, and a few religious rituals. Half-way through the service several children went to the front of the temple and rocked a cradle that had been placed there. In that moment, I was transported in time and space to another, familiar scene. Shepherds, wise men, angels and the congregation were worshiping a God child who had been born in a cradle to Mary and Joseph. The universality of a divine incarnation was brought home to me that day. We long so much for God to be with us that we place a cradle in the front of the church so that he can be born in the humblest manner among us. The Hindus in that sense are no different from Christians. They also celebrate the presence of the divine among us, in this case, the birth of their god Ram.

Is this the same religious rite, only expressed in different ways? I would suggest that this is not the case. We are not simply on different, parallel paths to the same God. More profound to me is the idea that the impetus for faith is similar. Let me give an example. The long line of islands in the West Indies came about as the result of volcanic eruptions from a single source. These islands are in a long line because the earth's plates shifted over a period of time as the eruptions took place. The reason for faith is the same, but the object and expression of it are different.

When I confess the infant child Jesus as Saviour and Lord, I embrace him as the manifestation of the very God self. This means that while I can identify with the Hindu celebration of the birth of their god Ram, I am not worshipping in the same way. My involvement with their services means that I am in solidarity with their need to practice their beliefs, but that does not mean that I believe in what they believe. The common belief of a god being born among us provides us with an entry point to dialogue across the gulf that separates us.

And she gave birth to her firstborn son and wrapped him in bands of cloth, and laid him in a manger, because there was no place for them in the inn (Luke 2:7).

8. *Enlightened Egalitarianism meets Hierarchical Monotheism*

Multi-faith worship events are delicate matters that have to take the particular aspects of each faith tradition into consideration. They provide a setting of mutual respect in which the larger public can participate. More negative fall-out than positive feedback sometimes occurs. Offering prayers in the legislature or during memorial services at major crash sites can cause more controversy than they are worth.

A similar mixed review occurred during a worship service at a national prison chaplaincy conference. The organizing committee wanted as many faith traditions represented as possible in the Morning Prayer services. They delegated these responsibilities to the various Christian, Islamic, Jewish, and Sikh traditions. The challenge for each group was to keep the integrity of their own religious practice while inviting others to participate in the prayers.

The result became particularly painful during the Islamic prayers. The Imam invited all those who wished to join him in offering prayers to Allah. Several chaplains felt led to participate. About twenty people came forward and began to kneel on the mats. As the participants lined up beside each other, the Imam asked the women to line up behind the men on the mats. One could feel the tension rising as the women chaplains complied with the request. What was to have been an act of solidarity with Islam suddenly turned into an embarrassing moment. These women felt they were re-living the life-long battle they had waged within their own denominations to be recognized as equal to men in spiritual leadership. Within a split second, that right had been taken away from them as they were asked to line up behind the men.

These women chaplains will be more guarded the next time they are asked to participate in an inter-faith religious service. Rituals have a way of getting away from us. We cannot anticipate all of the unspoken assumptions built into them. Is it any wonder that we are sometimes more satisfied with having no prayers at all? Running the gauntlet of unintended consequences as the result of well-meaning intentions is simply too tiring.

Then the king went to his palace and spent the night fasting; no food was brought to him, and sleep fled from him (Daniel 6:18).

9. Zoroaster, a Persian Prophet

The intrusion of foreign nations into my consciousness took place when I read the Babylonian encounters with the Israelites. Nebuchadnezzar had taken the Israelites into captivity because of his imperialistic ambitions along with their disobedience to God. Israel was a small vassal state under subservience to Persia. In spite of this fact, Cyrus and Darius declared that the Hebrews' God had dominion over the whole earth (Daniel 6:26-27). These kings sanctioned the building of a Jewish temple in Israel and let the exiles return to their homeland (Ezra and Nehemiah). The saviour of this story turns out to be an Iranian nation in the service of a Zoroastrian God.

This story takes a poignant, universal turn when one realizes that the sun is the central image of divinity for Zoroastrians. The Iranian New Year falls on the date of the spring Equinox, March 21st. God is like the sun in that God rules over the whole world. God provides the necessary warmth for human beings to sustain themselves. The planets revolve around the sun in the same way that religions revolve around God.

The fact that Cyrus and Darius declare the universality of the Hebrew God is important. It shows how the particularity of the gospel is manifested globally. This knowledge becomes especially important for chaplains who are trying to come to terms with the diversity of religious expressions within a prison context. Darius' confession facilitates a theoretical way beyond two alternatives. Faith is neither one among many nor a threat to the 'one and only' way. The universality of the gospel is manifest as part of the existence of the world (Acts 17, Romans 1). The celebration of the spring Equinox together with our aboriginal, Wiccan and Zoroastrian neighbours encourages us to celebrate the Son together with the Sun. A resurrection is announced at every dawn and a second coming at every setting. Every religion attaches itself to the universal manifestations of life in order to demonstrate its global efficacy.

The universal within the particular moves us beyond the nominalism of a God who is viewed phenomenally through many human forms. It was through the confession of a Hebrew God that Darius saved the people of Israel from exile. It is through the confession of a triune God that Christians help others understand the nature of God.

The Lord, the God of heaven, has given me all the kingdoms of the earth, and he has charged me to build him a house at Jerusalem in Judah (Ezra 1:2).

- Chapter Nine -

Restorative Justice

1. Painting the Electrical Pipe on the Outside of a Prison Wall

Chad, a man in his mid-thirties, came to me as I was facilitating a Bible study group one evening. He told me that he was finished with prison. I asked him what he meant. Chad told me that he had spent over ten years in prison. He was ready to lead a productive, law-abiding life.

We sat down and got to know each other better. Chad told me how he had escaped more than five times from various prisons. He told me how one night, in the middle of fog and a rain storm, he climbed over the barbed wire fence and escaped. A guard was standing only a few hundred feet away when he did this.

A year after this conversation, Chad was transferred to a minimum institution because of his good behaviour. He enrolled in a two year, meat-cutting course and completed it successfully. He applied for work release in the community. He was able to get some Escorted Temporary Absences. Chad re-established a relationship with his wife during this time.

One day, as I was going home, I noticed a man on a ladder that was propped up against the outside of the prison wall. I got closer and tried to figure out what he was doing there. I realized that it was Chad. I stopped the car, got out, and asked him what he was doing. Chad laughed, got down from the ladder, and gave me the following explanation. Prison officials found out how many times he had escaped. They thought the best way to test Chad's risk of escape would be to get him to paint the electrical pipe that ran around the top of the outside wall. He had been painting this pipe for the past two weeks. He had at least another two weeks to go. Every evening, Chad had to make the decision to go back into prison. He could do the easy thing and escape from this relatively unprotected area.

Chad smiled as he told me this story. He was grateful that he had to make this decision every day. He knew now, not only the price of freedom, but also the value of freedom. Chad's commitment to change five years earlier, along with his faith and community support, enabled him ultimately to return to society as a law-abiding citizen.

Thieves must give up stealing; rather let them labour and work honestly with their own hands, so as to have something to share with the needy (Ephesians 4:28).

2. Becoming Involuntarily Yoked to Each Other

When Naomi, my wife, and I bought our first duplex, we tore out the carpets and installed hardwood flooring before we moved in. After about a week of renovations, our Spanish neighbour came over and greeted us warmly. He spoke about the fact that living in a duplex is like becoming involuntarily yoked to each other. Everything that one person does affects the other person. It dawned on us what he, in his impeccable French and gentle manner, was trying to say to us. The noise we were making resounded loudly through the walls to their side of the duplex. We were unaware of how far sound traveled because we had not yet lived in the house.

This incident came to mind when Darrell spoke to me about his transfer to a minimum-security institution. As we began to talk, Darrell related to me the nature of his crime. It had happened over eight years ago. He spoke as though the event had happened yesterday. Darrell described in detail every aspect of the murder. It was at that moment that I realized that the perpetrator and victim in a metaphorical sense are involuntarily yoked to each other for the rest of their "lives." Darrell spoke as though the victim was still in the same room as we were, eight years after the tragedy had happened.

The same thing happened as I worked with Evan. He had committed a murder twenty years ago. New victim impact statements had been submitted and disclosed to him as a result of his request for parole. These statements made it clear that the events of twenty years ago were still fresh in the victims' minds. The victims were still suffering a great deal from what had happened.

After a violent crime, the victim and perpetrator are yoked together for "life". That event colours everything that happens afterward. It is like a marriage relationship turned sour. Evan is forced to live with his dead wife's memory for the rest of his life sentence. He was not able to unhook the marriage along with its emotional bonds peaceably through separation, divorce, or detachment. Evan chose to be attached violently to his wife's memory -- her life, her character, her love and her commitment. He was not able to allow the hateful emotions of the moment to be forgiven and healed. That is the tragedy of murder. Forgiveness seems to be only on the far horizon.

For I am convinced that neither death, nor life, nor angels, nor rulers . . . nor height, nor depth, nor anything else in all creation, will be able to separate us from the love of God in Christ Jesus our Lord (Romans 8:38-39).

3. Guilt by Association

A prison chaplain quickly finds out that associating with inmates is not the most popular thing to do. Several of the offenders I work with have had their pictures splashed on the front pages of newspapers. Their lives and crimes have been vilified. It is not easy to stand beside someone when one realizes the extent of harm they have caused other people.

The gravity of this situation became clear as I worked with Mario. Mario had served most of his sentence. He was eligible for Escorted Temporary Absences and had participated in them before. I suggested that I get permission for him to come and speak at our church. That proved the wrong thing to do. The members did not feel safe in having Mario come. They were upset that I had even suggested it. I had to come to terms with the fact that several members of the church had had experiences of abuse. They felt particularly vulnerable in this situation. I had no idea that such a simple suggestion could cause so much grief.

The same thing happened several years later when I began counselling Endrique about his estranged relationship with his wife. The question at hand had to do with contact with his children. It took less than a day and a phone call to his ex-wife's lawyer to make me realize the extent of animosity and fear that his former wife had of Endrique. Endrique had little understanding of the long term effects of the power, abuse, and manipulation he had used against his wife over many years. There was little I could do but apologize to her lawyer for having raised the subject at all.

These incidents made me realize that working with offenders is different from raising money for a children's charity. The extent of fear, harm, and rage that Mario and Endrique had caused was barely comprehensible to me. What I saw as sincere, motivated, transformed, and sober individuals was viewed quite differently by the people affected by their crimes.

Jesus had to go through similar experiences of rejection as he associated with people who were not seen as upstanding citizens in his culture. The animosity and conflict in the Gospel of John between Jesus and the Pharisees shows the extent to which Jesus was considered a threat and offence to others. This makes one realize what having compassion is all about.

All of them deserted him and fled (Mark 14:50).

4. Death Wishes, Remorse, and Forgiveness

The remorse that Julien had for his crime became evident when he shared his death wish with me. We were in the midst of discussing funeral arrangements for his father. A decision had to be made about where his father was going to be buried. Julien blurted out, "I wish it was me instead of my father who is being buried beside my grandfather."

Julien was able to speak about himself in these terms because we had spent many sessions talking about the circumstances and details of his offence. The awful nature of the crime made it especially difficult for me to come to grips with what Julien had done. We spent a lot of time reflecting on Julien's state of mind as he contemplated committing his offence. We spoke about his childhood, his challenges, and the reasons that he acted out in such a vicious manner. It took a year before I was able to understand, if not empathize with Julien's motives and actions.

Julien's statement that he wished that he could die in the place of his father marked a watershed. I realized the extent to which Julien vilified himself. He considered it perfectly acceptable for his victims to want him dead. Nothing could atone for the severity of harm and suffering and pain Julien had caused so many years ago. Nothing would ever take away the reality of innocent death that Julien had caused.

An odd thing happened during the time that I was working with Julien. A volunteer from the city in which Julien had lived came to me and asked if inmates ever expressed remorse. The reason she was asking was because one of her friends had experienced the murder of one of her relatives. I looked at the volunteer in astonishment. I wondered silently whether we were talking about the same event. I told her that I had just finished speaking with an inmate that morning, who told me that he was very sorry for what he had done.

I do not know if restorative justice was at work in these discussions. I do not think that the victims will ever feel relieved from what happened. They continue to live with the fact that they were random victims of an unprovoked attack. I would imagine that the sheer arbitrariness of the murder has made them continue to live in fear and dread.

Restorative justice is a process in which we are restored to God, self, and others. Julien has reached the first stage. He has accepted the fact that God has forgiven him. He has not, however, forgiven himself or been forgiven by his victims. These are things that will have to wait.

Be still and know that I am God! (Psalm 46:10)

5. *A Blank Sheet of Paper*

Graham came to me one day and asked me to fill out a spiritual inventory for him. This inventory was supposed to indicate where I thought Graham was on his spiritual journey. I hesitated in complying with Graham's request. I had gotten to know Graham over the past two years. He was a very sociable person, worked hard at his job, and was an asset to the chapel. Graham volunteered to help out wherever he was needed.

I had trouble filling out a spiritual inventory because Graham had a hard time speaking about anything personal. He mentioned his parents with whom he had been in touch years before. He mentioned some volunteers with whom he had been in correspondence. He made note of the fact that he had been recently recommended to go to a lower security facility.

Graham maintained a superficial relationship with these people. The picture Graham showed me of his parents had been taken more than ten years earlier. The volunteers were asked how much they knew about Graham. They indicated to the social worker that they had no knowledge of Graham's offences. Graham was transferred to a lower security institution. He was suspended after three months because of his inability to comply with community rules. Graham found it difficult to establish close social bonds.

In spite of my reservations, Graham continued to ask me to fill out a spiritual inventory. He told me that years ago, a chaplain at another institution had done one for him. His spiritual assessment needed to be updated. I indicated to him that I was not sure that I was capable of filling out this form. This was not something that I felt comfortable doing.

Graham would not take "no" for an answer. I went into my office, came back with a blank white sheet of paper, gave it to him, and said, "Here is your spiritual inventory." I could think of no other way of letting Graham know that he appeared incapable of dealing with life on a serious level.

It was only after the fact that I discovered the reason for Graham's superficial façade. He was facing quite a few more charges when he was released. He knew that if he started sharing about his life, he might reveal something for which he had not been convicted. Graham was protecting himself and me by keeping things on a superficial level. Superficiality is not a good basis for a real, honest spiritual inventory.

Keep your heart with all vigilance, for from it flow the springs of life (Proverbs 4:23).

6. The Lack of Emotion on a Prisoner's Face

The mother of a murdered son approached me during a victim-offender reconciliation conference. She asked me why the young seventeen year-old killer showed so little emotion as he stood behind the docket in the courtroom. Apparently, he had even bragged about the killing to his friends in the remand centre.

I realized the extent to which I had been institutionalized when I responded to her question. I meet inmates every day who show little if any emotion. They appear so hardened that one wonders if there is any way of getting through to them. In some cases, offenders have been so damaged that they feel as though they will explode if they reveal one more thing about their lives.

These men snap when someone looks at them the wrong way. These men will stab and kill the person beside them if they feel they have to. These men will not look around when they hear someone screaming. They could be implicated in the attack if they recognize the victim or culprit. These men will encourage an offender in the cell next to them to kill himself if he is feeling sorry for himself. This person may be in the "hole" because of his awful crime, because he has informed on someone else, or he has gotten himself into a lot of debt. These men cheer when a policeman is killed. What is to be said in the face of such hatred of life and satisfaction at another person's suffering and death?

These men act with so much bravado and daring because they have already lost almost everything. They have so little to live for that it does not seem to matter if they, or another person, are killed in the course of the "action." They have become empty shells within which, a heart is still beating.

These men are afraid to be vulnerable because they have been used and abused so many times in the past. They trust no one because the one person they depended on stomped all over them when they shared something personal. They show no emotion because this is the only way they know how to survive. What they need is new hearts.

I do not know if I answered the mother's question adequately. I do remember that I may have appeared somewhat callous in recounting my experience with offenders. I realized afterward that I had been influenced as much by their outlook on life as they by mine.

A new heart I will give you, and a new spirit I will put within you (Ezekiel 36:26).

7. On Dying Well

When Michelangelo was eighty years old, he sculpted a likeness of himself on the face of Nicodemus. This *Pieta del Duomo* shows Nicodemus, St. Joseph of Arimathea, and Mary Magdalene carrying Jesus' body to the grave. This is one of three *Pietas* that Michelangelo chiselled in his old age. His *Palestrina Pieta* shows Jesus' mother Mary looking on with concern and care as she and another person hold up his dead body. The *Pieta Rondanini* was left as an unfinished work depicting mother and her adult son.[50]

Interpreters have suggested that Michelangelo worked on these *Pietas* because of his own concern to "die well." Believers spent a lot of time during the Renaissance thinking about what it meant to die peaceably. For some, this meant receiving the sacrament of baptism at the same time as the "last rites." For others, it meant reflecting through art and writing on the death of Christ. Jesus' giving up of his spirit was seen as a model for the manner in which Christian believers could face and accept death.

Michelangelo's *Pietas* are suggestive of his faith. Nicodemus was a Pharisee who was spiritually re-born after his meeting with Jesus in the night. When Jesus died, Nicodemus brought myrrh and spices to prepare the body. Nicodemus saw the light -- something Jesus commented on during their first meeting (John 3:1-21, 10:39). Michelangelo's depiction of Nicodemus carrying Jesus was a way to demonstrate his own faith before he died.

The unfinished nature of Michelangelo's last *Pieta* is also suggestive of his view of death. Michelangelo worked and re-worked this piece for ten years before leaving it in its emaciated and open-ended form. Old age brings deformity and illness. One's belief in eternal life means that this earthly form is only the precursor to something else.

Inmates have a lot of time to ponder their mortal existence. Some prefer to end their life so that they can "be with" their murdered girlfriend or recently deceased uncle. Others soldier stoically on, believing that life is meaningful enough to be accepted. Still others find the wherewithal to be free within the existence in which they find themselves. This might mean the establishment of new relationships. In other cases, the body of believing Christians within prison is the best that can be expected.

The hope is that they, like we, may be like Simeon, who was content to die after he had seen Jesus. This feeling of peace in displacement may come at the birth of a child, at the end of a career, after a lifetime in prison, in an accident, after a long illness, or in the restfulness of sleep.

Master, now you are dismissing your servant in peace (Luke 2:29).

- Chapter Ten -

Ecclesiastical Implications of Chaplaincy

1. The Ideological Ramifications of Community

Programs such as Alternatives to Violence and the Christopher Leadership course are self-perpetuating. Participants actively recruit others once they have become convinced of the merits of the course. Opportunities are given for leadership through role playing. There is discussion of solutions to conflict. There are introductions of guest speakers. The engagement of participants empowers inmates to become leaders of their peers.

These programs differ from public speaking courses and "how to" workshops. Community facilitators offer personal sharing and faith perspectives. Quakers, deeply committed Christian pacifists, developed the Alternatives to Violence program. The Catholic Church formulated the Christopher Leadership course to encourage lay leadership within its parishes. These programs are non-denominational in content in order to reach out to the larger community. They are apologetic in the sense that they include features that correlate with the core beliefs of the initiating body.

One Christopher session is dedicated to the theme of community. A punch bowl serves as a common focal point. Each person is invited to take a glass of juice and explain the attributes they are bringing to community. They then pour this gift into the bowl. At the end of the session, the participants drink the combined juices and eat homemade bread. The similarity to communion is unmistakable.

This example reveals the strength and weakness of para-church programs. Their strength lies in their universal appeal. Everyone is for the ending of violence and the building up of community. Adding spiritual value to these courses sets them apart from "how-to" courses that are focused on short-term utilitarian goals. A sense of community is created as the participants work together.

A problem arises if religious rationales are named as the primary goal of the program. It would be inappropriate for participants to be invited to become a Quaker or a Catholic on the basis of these courses. The sustaining power of these programs is nevertheless rooted in their religious source.

All this is from God, who reconciled us to himself through Christ, and has given us the ministry of reconciliation (2 Corinthians 5:18).

2. *Religious Identity and Universal Appeal*

All para-church organizations work with the dynamic of religious identity and universal appeal. "Alpha" is an introductory course to Christianity that is offered to non-believers. Everything works fine until religious rites of passage come into play. The founders of Alpha explain the Anglican sources of their inspiration. The Catholic Church offers a follow-up course for new believers entitled, "Catholicism 201."

A recent "Pursuit of Happiness Course," entitled *Criminon,* has been successfully introduced into prison. Many offenders are looking for a spiritually-directed course that does not have religious implications. Upon reading the fine print, one realizes this course is a spin-off of Ron Hubbard's parapsychological musings of the 1960s known as Scientology. Similar examples include genealogical organizations that have their roots in Mormonism or vegetarian groups that come from Seventh-Day Adventism. Daily diaries that have Sunday as the first day of the week are supplied by the Lord's Day Association.

These illustrations are pertinent to my own identity as a chaplain. As an ordained minister of the Mennonite Church, I am hired to serve as a chaplain to all Protestants in the institution. I am also hired to facilitate other religious groups as well as to work ecumenically with chaplains of different faith traditions. A question that arises is whether prison chaplaincy would be better off having no denominational affiliation at all.

A broad, spiritual approach has been instituted in many hospitals. I recently asked for the pastoral care department so I could speak with a hospital chaplain. I was told that the hospital is dedicated to spiritual care and its practitioners are known as spiritual caregivers.

These illustrations raise the issue of religious identity. Should we require ecclesiastical boundary markers to delineate our visible adherence? Or would it be better to provide a broad spiritual approach that minimizes our religious moorings? I believe that holding these two poles in a dynamic balance is the most fruitful solution. The universal appeal of religion and spirituality makes us think about what our particular faith traditions have to contribute.

It was in Antioch that the disciples were first called "Christians" (Acts 11:26).

3. *Where is the Christian Worship Service?*

Joseph came to the chapel one Sunday evening just before I was going to begin the worship service. He looked disgruntled when he glanced at the liturgical order of worship that had been printed. He asked somewhat facetiously, "Where is the Christian worship service taking place?" I replied in kind, with the same tongue-in-cheek attitude, "Two doors down, and on your right." Joseph felt that the worship service had become so ritualized that it was no longer meaningful.

Joseph had difficulty in accepting a set worship style. He had learned the truth of the Bible and faith on his own, without the intervention of another authority or expert. He preferred to read his Bible and pray on a daily basis in his cell. He did not feel comfortable coming to the chapel and worshiping with other believers. The hypocrisy of the church was a stumbling block for Joseph. He would rather spend his time listening to the sermons of television evangelists.

It is hard for me to comment on this perceived self-righteousness. I am glad that some offenders are nurturing their faith in Christianity in spite of the chaplains' best efforts. Several men feel that we as chaplains are so much part of the system that we have little or no credibility left. We appear to cater to "every need" without setting firm limits on what is acceptable within Christianity. The idea that we can facilitate many types of spirituality without compromising our faith is not understandable to some believers. Rigid thinking is often what has resulted in offenders coming to prison in the first place. We as chaplains are reticent to establish too many hard and fast rules.

This reticence may be misguided. My preference is to set clear boundaries regarding certain aspects of faith. Real faith has to be nurtured in a safe atmosphere before it can mature into something extraordinary. It is like a parent providing space for the child to internalize his or her own rules and authority. The parent provides sufficient external boundary markers to help the child steer clear of the most dangerous avalanches and accidents.

But this I admit to you, that according to the Way, which they call a sect, I worship the God of our ancestors (Acts 24:14).

4. *Being Baptized into the Universal Body of Jesus Christ*

The daughter of the minister in the church in which I grew up asked to be baptized into the "invisible body of Jesus Christ." She felt more comfortable with this possibility than associating too closely with the human foibles that she observed in the congregation of which we were a part.

This issue has stayed with me during my years as a minister and chaplain. The first thing that many new believers in prison ask is whether they can be baptized. When I hem and haw, they cite the Ethiopian's reply to Philip, "Look, here is water! What is to prevent me from being baptized?" (Acts 8:36). Several Pentecostal ministers with whom I work would be more than happy to facilitate this process if I said yes. Several chaplain colleagues baptize prisoners upon their confession of faith in Jesus Christ.

Linking baptism to church membership is the biggest difference that I see between the Mennonite church and some other evangelical denominations. I believe that prisoners have to become members of a particular church body if they are going to be baptized. This means that they have to be "catechized" and recommended by a congregation in order for me to move ahead with baptism.

This places me in the odd position of being closer to the policies of some mainline churches that practice infant baptism than some Protestant denominations that adhere to believers' baptism. The Anglican and Catholic traditions insist on the church membership of the parents before the priests will baptize their infants. The same often holds for marriages. The bride and groom have to decide to which church they want to belong before a priest will marry them. Discussion of religious preferences before marriage saves a lot of grief for the couple when they are getting their children baptized.

Setting religious boundaries to profound spiritual experiences appears to me to be a better way of proceeding than blessing everything that comes along. In the heartfelt moment, I want to confirm a religious conversion or spiritual awakening with something more than a prayer and the laying on of hands. I want to invoke the power of the Spirit and baptize with water as well. I nevertheless have found it ultimately more satisfying to provide adequate preparation for what I regard as a sacrament of the church.

Can anyone withhold the water for baptizing these people . . . ? (Acts 10:47)

5. *Changed by the Sacredness of Communion*

I knew I was on the right track when I first celebrated communion in prison. I was presiding over the sacrament in a Catholic chapel in the midst of Christian, Hindu, Sikh, and Islamic believers. After a year of ministry there, it was time to institute this sacred aspect of our Christian faith. How else to proclaim the community of believers except through an affirmation of the body to which we belonged?

I felt comfortable celebrating communion because of the way in which the inmates responded. The offenders who proclaimed Christ as Saviour and Lord stepped forward and stood in a small semi-circle around the altar. It felt as though they were being guided by an unseen hand. The inmates from other faith traditions formed an outer semi-circle around this small Christian group. They understood what it meant to respect the sacredness of a ritual of a different faith. As everyone participated in the prayers of confession, petition, and thankfulness, the Christians received the bread and cup in honour of their God. What more did I have to say? The invisible had been made visible.

This rich experience of communion has continued to follow me as I have celebrated the Eucharist in other institutions. In some institutions, the only inmates who refuse communion are the ones who know something about what it means. In other facilities, the Christian volunteers question me about its appropriateness. They know something about what it means to be a collective visible body of Jesus Christ.

My first communion inside prison was so moving because I came from a tradition where closed communion was celebrated twice a year on a Sunday evening. The bread and cup were distributed so seldom because of their integral link to a redeemed body of believers. Preparation sermons were preached for two Sundays so believers had time to make amends with their fellow Christians (1 Corinthians 11:27-32). Communion services were held in the evening so that morning worshippers were not caught unawares about what was happening.

These preparation sermons were so effective that fewer and fewer people felt qualified to partake of communion. After the numbers had dwindled to fewer than twenty people, the pastor decided to change his theology in order to celebrate communion. I have had to do the same thing.

This cup is the new covenant in my blood (1 Corinthians 11:25).

6. Serving Communion in an Appropriate Manner

Adrienne Clarkson, the former Governor General of Canada, attended a Mass presided over by the Catholic Archbishop when she visited Quebec. A newspaper article described how she, as part of the Anglican Church, was given a special dispensation to receive communion during the service. The article went on to discuss the relative merits of allowing members of different denominations to receive communion at the hands of a Catholic priest.

This incident stuck in my mind. I was going through a similar period of discernment in serving communion in the institution. Attendance in the service had dropped off to a few participants. More often than not, they came for the fellowship and coffee instead of the prayers and the Eucharist. The sincerity of the men was so much in doubt that I decided to forgo serving communion until one of them asked for it. I was surprised by the response. It took six months before one of the men came forward and asked why I had not had a communion service recently. I spent the next Sunday service explaining my understanding of the gathered community of Christian believers. I told them that the church was a visible presence represented in the body and blood of Christ.

This incident demonstrated how elusive it is for a communion of believers to be in touch with the Holy Spirit, rooted in their dependence on Christ, and committed to following God. I have noticed the ebbs and flows of a visible body of believers within prison throughout the twenty years of my ministry. Euphoria has ruled on some occasions. More often than not, we have had to find a special dispensation to partake of the body in order not to offend the sensibilities of those involved. The burdens on our consciences have had to be doubly confessed to receive the absolution that is available. Our prayers are heart-felt on these occasions. We struggle to see ourselves as sufficiently bound to the body of Christ. Perhaps this is why the special dispensation that Adrienne Clarkson received meant so much to me. There are at least some occasions when the unified visible body can be honoured.

Then their eyes were opened, and they recognized him (Luke 24:31).

7. *Women as Priests and Pastors*

I realized the extent to which women in leadership is still an issue when I asked Amanda, an Anglican priest, to replace me while I went on vacation. Amanda reported back to me that the inmates in the congregation had a hard time accepting her religious authority. They made personal passes to her as a woman and were generally unruly in behaviour. Administration had questioned her role as a priest and had raised issues about her safety. I also learned that Lillian, one of the regular woman volunteers, had refused to play piano for Amanda because she did not believe that a woman in pastoral leadership was biblical.

This situation made me aware of how much gender affects everything. I had to reflect on the time it took me to accept Marion as my pastor in our church. I shared with Marion differently from the way that I had confided in Doug, the previous pastor. I realized that past experiences of male-female friendships played a role in the way that I related to Marion. I had to own these feelings in order to accept her as my pastoral confidant, professional colleague, and ecclesiastical authority.

I also had to own the fact that I considered the Enlightenment philosophy of equality to be an important factor in my interpretation of scripture. Paul's claim that there is neither male nor female in Christ (Galatians 3:28-29) trumped his advice in 1 Corinthians 11:10 about women wearing veils in church. It also undercut Paul's remarks in 1 Timothy 2:12 that say that women have no authority over a man. The women's suffrage movement in the early part of the 20th century has proven that a woman can be as powerful and authoritative in her faith and leadership as a man. I saw no reason for women to be excluded from pastoral and priestly leadership within the church.

This stance was at odds with Lillian's beliefs. She belonged to the Plymouth Brethren Church that did not believe in women in leadership. To her credit, Lillian always wore a head covering as a sign of respect. She took Paul's words literally in 1 Corinthians 11:2-16.

The rationale I used with the inmates when I got back from my vacation was the following. "Even James Bond has a woman boss at the head of British Intelligence Service. You had better get used to the idea of taking directions from a woman."

For all of you are one in Christ Jesus (Galatians 3:28).

8. *Engaged in Evangelism*

I arrived at the chapel every Sunday evening at six p.m. to prepare for my seven o'clock worship service. From my office window, I could see five men standing two hundred yards away under a shelter near the baseball field. They had established this group meeting as part of a Sunday evening ritual. By the time seven o'clock arrived, they were nowhere to be seen.

This routine went on for three months. I decided one evening to forgo my evening preparation to visit them. They were cordial in their welcome and interested in what I had to say. When I asked them about the worship services, they indicated that they did not feel welcome. The services had been conducted in French for some time. The English population was small and divided along ethnic lines. The fact that they were from Jamaica and Barbados did not help the situation.

To my surprise, they showed up at the next Protestant service. It was clear that they were Christians from the way that they sang and participated in the prayers. While feeling a little alienated, they began to drop by my office and speak to me about the circumstances that brought them to jail. I had no idea what difference a small gesture could make. All I had done was walk over to their enclave and introduce myself.

This little incident changed the way I did ministry. From then on, I made a point of introducing myself to as many people as possible. The lone person in the corner was probably as interested in being accepted by me and God as the rest of the people there. We are all shy in asking for help. Sometimes, it takes the other person to reach out his or her hand first.

The chapel services became the most integrated and the most dynamic of all the services which I have led. We had sermons simultaneously translated into two languages during the course of the worship. Pentecostal volunteers were the most adept at knowing what needed to be said to the residents. Drama and mime became a normal part of acting out the gospel story. Testimonies were offered on a weekly basis. There was a general feeling of camaraderie that has stayed with me. These events occurred more than fifteen years ago.

Blessed be the God and Father of our Lord Jesus Christ, who has blessed us in Christ with every spiritual blessing (Ephesians 1:3).

- Chapter Eleven -

Theological Reflections

1. Getting One's Theology Right

One of the chief worries that Loren had when I offered a seven-step spiritual journey course was that I did not have my theology right. He sat beside me with his Bible open in case he had to cross-reference something I said. I smiled inwardly as I began the course. I felt some satisfaction as Loren slowly relaxed during the third session and concluded that what I was speaking about was not all bad.

A similar experience happened to me during one of my worship services. I was speaking on something I knew would be controversial. Sure enough, halfway through my meditation, Peter, one of the regular attendees, got up and left. He told me later that he was not sure that I was orthodox enough for his liking.

These two incidents remind me of how firm a foundation inmates need to stand on. Both of these men had their trust broken and their lives turned upside down at a young age. They grew up confused and committed their crimes as a result of their misconstrued view of reality. When they discovered Jesus, they hung on to the Book for dear life. They were ready to question anyone who deviated from what they viewed as fundamental.

These two experiences led me to believe that getting one's theology straight is not an easy task. The world was skewed the moment Loren and Peter were born. They have been searching ever since for a straight plumb line (Amos 7:8) by which they can measure their abusive and dysfunctional upbringing. By listening to their story, I was able to identify the underlying emotions, views, beliefs, and patterns of behaviour that predisposed them to particular scriptural passages.

Dave felt that he could never be forgiven because he had "fallen away from his faith" and "blasphemed the Holy Spirit" (Hebrews 6:6, Mark 3:29).

Sam emphasized the importance of speaking the truth because he had been deceived and lied to for most of his life (Psalm 15:2). Ted was continually claiming the assurance of faith because of his doubt about God's love (Hebrews 11:22). Byron "hoped against hope" that he would be released because there was so little chance of this ever happening (Romans 4:18). Nurturing these scriptures within a context of safety and understanding of their unique struggles provided a forum for these offenders to express their fundamental theology in an appropriate manner.

But the aim of such instruction is love that comes from a pure heart (1Timothy 1:5).

2. More Righteous than the Pope

One of the odd things that happen to offenders when they become converted to the gospel is that they start acting more religious than the chaplains. They quote scripture every chance they get. They tell us what the original meaning of a word is in Hebrew or Greek. They inform the priest who comes in to say Mass exactly how the altar should be arranged.

It took me a while to understand the reasons for this phenomenon. Sometimes, the amount of religiosity that offenders displayed appeared to be inversely proportional to the seriousness of the crimes they committed. Inmates are often ostracized for their offences and ranked according to the nature of their crimes. The lower on the totem pole they fall, the more likely it is that they will be found in the chapel. They take Bible studies by correspondence and speak to chaplains about their conversion experiences.

There are at least two reasons for this type of conversion experience. The first is that inmates are seeking a safe haven from the persecution they are facing from other inmates. Offenders at the top of the hierarchical order according to the inmate code internalize society's harsh attitudes toward men who have committed crimes against women and children. They mete out this punishment upon the most vulnerable within prison. It is no wonder that inmates who have committed these types of crimes often go through a genuine conversion experience.

A second, more profound reason has to do with the offenders' guilt and shame. The depth of sin to which they have sunk has made them rebound on the other side of righteousness to make up for the terrible harm they have caused. Their overt and sometimes annoying religiosity is a type of "works righteousness" by which they hope to earn their salvation and appease the wrath of God.

I became more attuned to what the offenders were really trying to tell me as they shared their testimonies and Biblical knowledge. Their religiosity diminished as we were able to speak about their fears, hopes, dreams, and faith -- as well as the offences they had committed. In the safety of divine acceptance, they were able to like themselves more as well as to be at ease enough to act like themselves. They no longer had to wear a mask to cover up the multitude of sins for which they had been convicted.

But those who do what is true come to the light, that it may be clearly seen that their deeds have been done in God (John 3:21).

3. *Cursing in Different Languages*

I had no idea how attached Quebec people were to their church. I listened to them curse with abandon, using such words as *hostie, tabernacle, sacrament, Mon Dieu,* and *sacre bleu.* These words refer to different elements of the Mass. The body of Christ, the *host,* is kept within the *tabernacle,* a tent of the holy presence of God that the Israelites built in the wilderness. The church is blessed by *Mon Dieu* the Father, and offered to the congregation in the form of a *sacrament.* Who would have thought that such sacred expressions of faith could be turned into words of disdain and disrespect?

I reflected on the curse words that were used by English Protestants. I began to understand the love-hate relationship that people have with deeply ambiguous aspects of their lives. French people are surprised when they learn the extent to which Anglo-Saxon Protestants curse about sex. The French person wonders: Why would someone use so many negative sexual expressions? Sex is great! Why curse something you love?

The curse words used by these two cultures made me understand the role of taboos in our society. Heaven and hell, love and sex, hosts and tabernacles represent that which both fascinates and frightens us. Fear of hell can chase us into heaven. Fear of sex can lead us to be very uptight about the desires we have as furtive human beings. The taboo that is uttered in a curse word reveals the extent to which we are controlled by that desire. Sexual pre-occupation can come to a point where we use a sexual curse word in every other sentence.

Fear of the priest and the power of the church led the French Catholic community to vilify and denigrate all aspects of the Mass. It was not until the Quiet Revolution of the 1960s that the power of the church was replaced by a belief in nationalism. French people could finally be liberated to exchange their religious curse words for political ones. I do not know if that was an improvement, but it demonstrates how taboos change over time.

It is better to light one candle than curse the darkness (Christopher saying).[51]

4. Resident Alien

One of my family members from Canada was accepted to work in the United States of America. He was referred to as a "resident alien" on his identity card. This word jumped out at me because of its long history within the biblical literature. Abraham refers early on to himself as a "resident alien" (Genesis 23:4). He is dependent on the Hittite king to obtain a plot of land to bury his wife, Sarah. The books of the law (Leviticus 25) go on to welcome the strangers and sojourners who wander with the Israelites to the land of Canaan. They are to be reckoned as one of the chosen people. They are circumcised to indicate membership in the divine covenant. A final commentary on alienated people occurs at the end of the book of Hebrews. Jesus is referred to as a lamb that is sacrificed outside the camp. The book of Hebrews goes on to make the following suggestion (13:13-14):

"Let us then go to him outside the camp and bear the abuse he endured. For here we have no lasting city, but we are looking for the city that is to come."

My ancestors from Eastern Europe were tag-alongs as the Mennonites crossed from the Netherlands to Prussia and on to Russia. They became grafted onto the Anabaptist faith, even though they were originally Catholics. Tracing one's roots to get a sense of identity and belonging sometimes ends up with the realization that we are all sojourners seeking a homeland where we can put down roots.

These biblical reflections have become pre-occupations for me because of my involvement with marginalized peoples. They often appear to me as one-dimensional beings with so little history and attachments that they have a hard time putting their lives into perspective. They are like prickly burrs that attach themselves to the first thing that comes along. Rootedness is hard to come by.

At the same time, a story of redemption can emerge from such a transient existence. Israel became a nation after forty years in the wilderness. The goodwill of those around them kept them upright. Some of us hang onto this world and its attachments too tightly. We never learn what it is like to let go and depend on God and others.

So then you are no longer strangers and aliens, but you are citizens with the saints and also members of the household of God (Ephesians 2:19).

5. Peace and Prosperity Gospel

Offenders are impressed with the glossy colour calendars along with the Bibles, daily readings, and Victory magazines that are put out by Kenneth Copeland Ministries. The smiling faces of Kenneth and Gloria along with their family on nearly all of the twelve month picture slots make the inmates feel as though they belong vicariously to a warm and loving family.

Kenneth's gospel of healing and prosperity is appreciated just as much. The book of Hebrews says that we are to own the victory and confidence that Christ gives us by approaching the throne of grace and claiming what is rightfully ours (4:16; 10:19-23). That claim, according to Kenneth Copeland, has specifically to do with miraculous healing and a financial prosperity that is craved by many within a prison environment.

Kenneth leads by example. He displays a Lear Jet that he has just bought so that he can reach the mission field faster. Kenneth claims that 10% of the donations he receives goes into direct ministry programming. Ken views the charitable giving that he receives as revenue, of which 10% goes toward actual ministry. Is that a miracle of immense proportions?

Kenneth Copeland is viewed with such devotion because of the pain that offenders experience. For them, only a miracle will do! They have tried many other measures and failed miserably at them. All that is left is a Hail Mary! in which inmates hope to catch a "long bomb" (football metaphor) that some one has thrown them. There is often little rationality or common sense in their reactions to the many different situations in which they find themselves.

Dylan, an offender who understands suffering better than most, recently commented to me that the message of Jesus is no "peace and prosperity gospel." This gentleman recently lost his wife, family, possessions, and country in which he had lived for forty years. Dylan spoke his words with some bitterness. He has nevertheless found solace in the forgiveness, mercy, love, compassion, and long-suffering nature of God. Through the tough face of stubbornness can be seen a man who understands the reasons why he has lost everything and accepts these losses as his own. He knows intimately what it is like to suffer and be sacrificed outside the camp. He has claimed the salvation of Jesus in order for his own stripes to be healed. He is finding his prosperity in acceptance and belonging within a fellowship of believers and with God.

Let us therefore approach the throne of grace with boldness, so we may receive mercy and find grace to help in time of need (Hebrews 4:16).

6. Three Ways to Stop a Conversation

We have a saying among the colleagues with whom I work. "There are three ways to stop a conversation. You can say (1) "I am a socialist," (2) "I am from Quebec," or (3) "I work with sex offenders." Any one of these statements will cause a moment of silence. The conversation will then switch to a safer topic.

The reason for this polite switch to other topics is that we do not have a sphere of reference by which to make small talk about these issues. It reminds me of the time I worked as a chaplain in the hospital. I spoke about everything but death to the dying person in front of me. Finally, the kind lady said, "Don, please pay attention to what I am saying. I am dying. I need someone to pray with me right now. I need the courage to die in peace and in the arms of Jesus." She died the next day while I was on my way to visit her.

We have to help others with spheres of reference in addition to the content of our faith. The most progressive person I met in the United States during my two-year sojourn there could not fathom that we in Canada allowed socialized medicine. "That's communism," the young city doctor told me. That was supposed to settle the argument. He could not imagine that the line-ups in the hospital that he had just finished showing me could be solved in any other manner than through private largesse.

The question remains: "Can we find a reference point outside our own reality? Can it keep us on the straight and narrow path of faith and righteousness?" I would suggest two examples from history. The first is the Confessing Church in Germany during World War II. In the face of severe opposition, it confessed that the German Church had compromised its faith. Hitler's actions were contrary to God. The second illustration comes from the 19th century Civil War in the United States. Lincoln stood on the historic truth that slavery was wrong. Many people could not see the gospel light of that statement.

These examples give us hope that we are not fated to be blinded by our own "truths" to the detriment of the gospel. Each social, political, and religious position requires the wrestling of active engagement and contemplative reflection in the silence of our hearts and the cauldron of Christian community to remain true to God's purposes.

There is no longer Jew or Greek, there is no longer slave or free, there is no longer male or female; for all of you are one in Christ Jesus (Galatians 3:28).

7. Jesus Behind Bars

A large black and white drawing of "Jesus behind bars" hangs in the chapel area. Jesus is standing with his left hand grasping a vertical bar. Thorns are on his head. A crosspiece of the metal shafts imprints a shadow on his cheek. He is looking serene, pensive, and caring. It is hard to tell which side of the fence he is on. Is he a chaplain listening to the viewer's story or is the viewer offering solace in Jesus' time of need?

The idea that Jesus spent a night behind bars comes from the fact that Jesus was arrested in the evening and tried in the morning (Luke 22:63-66). Jesus spent some time in the courtyard of the high priest, as well as in the praetorium of Pilate (John 18:28). There may have been a holding cell in either of these two places.

This picture is powerful because inmates can identify with Jesus' arrest, scourging, and crucifixion. They, too, have been sentenced and punished. An emotional bond with this Jesus is established. We can identify with Jesus because he first identified with us (Hebrews 4:15).

We identify with this picture because it shows how suffering can be redemptive. Inmates ask themselves what good can come from the harm they have done and punishment they have received. They want to be able to make amends for what they have done. The suffering that they see in the picture helps make their own suffering more bearable.

The suffering and death that Jesus endured is redemptive in a way that our suffering is not. The innocent lamb that was slaughtered was a way for deserved sin and punishment to be cancelled. The punishment for our sin has already been completed. We look to Jesus who took on our sins and suffered for our sakes. This is what gives meaning to human punishment and gives it the power to transform.

For . . . while we were enemies, we were reconciled to God (Romans 5:10).

8. *Facing the Window of Hope*

There was a time when I became discouraged in my prison ministry. I had worked three years to establish procedures for the ritual practices of various minority faith groups. Everything was suspended when food entered the institution through surreptitious means. Inmates found a means of having shrimp and steak delivered for Christmas. A religious representative provided some extra meals that had not been approved. I was told that I would have to start all over. These procedures needed to be written up as Standing Orders.

Several inmates were using the chapel as a place for gang recruitment. They were passing on contraband to their friends. They found the chapel to be a safe place where they could carry on their non-religious activities. I had to work hard to separate "the wheat from the chaff."

My office served as a poignant reminder of the challenges I faced. My desk literally faced a blank wall that was about 9 feet high. I found myself becoming more and more melancholy as I sat in my desk chair day after day.

I realized that this state of affairs had to change. I spent a week rearranging my office to rectify the situation. I moved the desk so that it faced the door. It was now situated between the offender and me as we talked. This arrangement created distance and distracted us from the conversation at hand.

Finally, I moved the desk beside the window that looked out onto a small patch of grass, sky, and the abutting building. I found this arrangement to be much better. There was something about an open space through a wall that lightened my spirits and enlivened my ministry. Even though the window could not be used as a door, the light from the outside illuminated the problems on the inside. The fact that I could literally see through a wall enabled me to face the challenges of my role with courage and dignity.

I have subsequently arranged my desk to face the window in every institution in which I have worked. I have found freedom to choose a way of being in my work that nurtures hope.

As the Father has sent me, so I send you (John 20:21).

9. Guarding the Portals of Human Desires

The people of Israel had to pass between two mountains when they crossed the Jordan River and made their way to Jericho under the leadership of Joshua. Six representatives of the tribes of Israel stood on Mount Gerazim, which was the mountain of blessing. Six representatives stood on Mount Ebal, which was the mountain of curses. The people were able to cross into the land of Canaan once the appropriate sacrifices had been made (Deuteronomy 27:1-14).

When I preach on this passage, I ask the congregation: On which mountain did God command Israel to erect an altar and make sacrifices? Was it on the mountain of blessings or on the mountain of curses?

I am always struck by the biblical answer to this question. Contrary to what one might think, God asked Israel to set up twelve large stones on Mount Ebal, the mountain of curses. Joshua was asked to write the words of the law clearly on these stones. The altar was erected on Mount Ebal because the taboos of human nature need to be guarded with a law and an altar so that we do not sin. Max Weber would call this the need for external authority. This is what a prison is, writ large. Offenders have been put into prison because they have not been able to exercise their conscience or control their inner nature.

It sometimes feels as though prison staff are sacrificing daily on the altar of Mount Ebal so that curses will not come raining down upon us or the rest of society. Blessings are easy. They overflow with abundance and plenty and joy and are celebrated as such. It is the curses we worry about. They take up much more space and time and energy (cf. Deuteronomy 28). We need a lot of staff to guard the entrance to these portals of human desire. It is only as we master these tendencies through the authority of Jesus Christ that we can move on to live in the land of milk and honey.

Therefore obey the Lord your God, observing his commandments and his statutes that I am commanding you today (Deuteronomy 27:10).

10. Guarding the Portals of Divine Mystery

The birth and death of Jesus are of such importance that the Christian church has safeguarded these liminal experiences in theological terms. The virgin birth and miraculous resurrection stand at the limits of history in order to sanctify the "real history" of Jesus' life.

The Catholic Church goes further by declaring that the Virgin Mary was immaculately conceived and assumed into heaven. The stain of sin is so strong that the Catholic Church has declared the birth of Mary to be sinless. The Church has proclaimed the assumption of Mary to show that she was not touched by the "pangs of mortal death." Jesus Christ and Mary have been declared immaculate from the corruptible influences of human history.

The New Testament is oriented from the start toward Christian apologetics about the divinity of Jesus. The wise men are moved to fall at the feet of the young child Jesus and worship him (Matthew 2:11). The Roman centurion who sees Jesus die can only confess: "Truly, this man was God's Son!" (Mark 15:39).

The Catholic Church guards the portal of the Eucharist in the same way. Only male celibate priests after the order of Jesus' apostles can ask God to turn the wine and bread into the body and blood of Jesus. Explicit taboos are necessary to make the sacrament work.

A similar example is available from the secular world. Howard Hughes started washing his hands constantly when he became paranoid about the dangers of disease. When his fears did not abate, he hired seven Mormon believers to safeguard his meals and monitor his communication with the outside world. Mormon taboos about food convinced Hughes that they were the best staff to keep his life safe. Similar taboos are at work in the theological justification of Jesus' divinity and the Catholic Church's tight rules regarding the blessing and distribution of the Eucharist.

How are these theological reflections relevant for prison ministry? Chaplains spend a lot of time thinking about how they can incorporate the sacredness of life within a setting that dehumanizes and denigrates people. Taking the time to listen along with making space to reflect provides the wherewithal to set spiritual limits to the encroaching world. Who knows what Word we need to hang on to in order to make our day worthwhile? Who knows what gesture is appropriate to make contact with the divine? I make myself slow down to savour the moment in which the divine is present in between the cracks of time. This is analogous to the amount of time the Bible and the church devote to making Jesus sacred.

Look, the virgin shall conceive and bear a son (Matthew 1:23, cf. Isaiah 7:14).

11. Two and Three Dimensional Realities

Puzzle makers some years ago discovered a way to hide a three-dimensional picture underneath a two-dimensional abstract mosaic. The viewer had to concentrate on a spot in the middle of the two-dimensional work. Slowly, the hidden three-dimensional perspective emerged.

A theological implication of this way of seeing is that we need to escape the two-dimensional reality of the mundane world in order to embrace a rich, virtual reality. Playing video games and watching television are examples of three-dimensional escapism. They enable a means of relief by which we do not have to face the everyday problems of our lives. Unfortunately, living in suspended time offers only temporary relief. Avoidance through denial and drugs is effective for only so long before we have to face the reality in front of us.

A better way of seeing God's presence in the world is to imagine a work of art as a two-way mirror. A light shines back at us as we attempt to grasp the meaning of a painting. This is what the medieval artists had in mind when they painted icons in a deliberately flat, two-dimensional perspective. The flat surface of an icon reflects the divine mystery within the painting onto the world that is in front of the viewer.

Max Weber uses a variety of sociological terms to describe this experience.[52] Members of a cloister are engaged in other-worldly asceticism when they devote their service to the divine. Catholic worker priests who serve the poor are this-worldly ascetics reminiscent of Calvinists and their work ethic. This-worldly asceticism helps us think of God as One who engages our lives. God is not a three-dimensional virtual object to whom we can escape. The personal, emotive, pietistic, and devotional practices we engage in are only as good as the fruit they produce in our lives. This is why television and entertainment can be so numbing. This is why worship and repose can be so refreshing. The former merely transports us while the latter has the potential to transform us.

And the Word became flesh and lived among us, and we have seen his glory, the glory as of a father's only son, full of grace and truth (John 1:14).

12. Salvation as Tragedy

Reinhold Niebuhr has made the point that crucifixion is the only way that the love of Christ enters history.[53] Christ stands at the edge of history because human beings can not stand the perfectionism that Jesus represents. The tragedy of Christ's death is the most that we can hope for in terms of a redeemed life.

I have had a chance to ponder this limited view of salvation within a prison context. The spectre of death and destruction epitomized by the prisoners' offences makes a person pause in the face of such evil. As a mediator of restorative justice recently told me, "Some acts are unspeakable."

Reinhold Niebuhr is suggesting that the most that can be hoped for is a forgiveness of these offenders' sins. Words of redemption, sanctification, holiness, and righteousness pale before the justification that Christ's death represents. This view has merit. I remember Pope John Paul II forgiving the person who tried to assassinate him. In spite of the forgiveness rendered, the offender remained behind bars as a consequence of his actions. The dynamic of the wrath and love of God remains active in human history.

One of the limitations of Niebuhr's Augustinian view of grace is that it offers little hope. For Niebuhr, the resurrection is only a dim light that may or may not be visible. I have had to consider the good that is an inherent part of our being. Hope is what adds spark to fuel. Salvation as a result of *agape* is more capable of sanctification than Niebuhr would have us believe. The good that God would have us be ultimately overcomes the evil that pulls us down and makes hypocrites of ourselves. This way of speaking about the goodness of God and the world moves us beyond Niebuhr's ultimately pessimistic view of human nature and destiny.

We must remember that Reinhold Niebuhr lived in the midst of a tumultuous time of American history. After anguishing discussions about the United States' role in the world, he convinced his country to enter World War II in order to stop Germany. Sanctification is not a word that one would use to describe this victory. "Justification" of this war is more appropriate. May we be as wise in knowing how to use the words of justification and sanctification when speaking about the transformation that we see in offenders.

Therefore we have been buried with him by baptism into death, so that . . . we too might walk in newness of life (Romans 6:4).

13. The Will of the Father and the Will of the Son

Inmates are drawn to the authority of the Father because they have failed at so many things. The unbridled assertion of their wills has ended in tragedy and heartache time after time. They are ready to try something else. The Will of the Father is an attractive method by which inmates hope they can turn their lives around.

I am reminded of Luther's discussion of the relationship between human and divine will. He suggests that human beings are like wild horses that need to be bridled, broken and tamed in order to serve a godly purpose. Our only task is to choose whether we want God or Satan to harness us. All other decisions need to be left up to God.

I am drawn to this dramatic account of salvation because it fits with my experience of life. I have had three careers, lived in three different provinces, and been blessed with a wonderful family. I have had to let Christ become the master and lord of my life in order for ministry to happen.

This dynamic experience of God's rule has made me appreciate a "*Christus Victor*" view of atonement. This approach sees Jesus Christ engaged in a dramatic battle against the forces of evil. The whole armour of God is enlisted to fight the wiles of the devil. Death and sin have been wrestled to the ground and placed under the feet of the conquering Jesus. I can identify with this need to let Christ wrestle with my life and place it under his control.

The question of how much our will plays a part in our salvation remains. Jesus' responses to the Father in the Gospel of John are helpful in this regard. Jesus declares that he "has the power to lay down his life and the power to take it up again" (John 10:18). The soldiers in the Garden of Gethsemane fall to the ground when Jesus retorts that "I am he" (John 18:6). Jesus lectures Pilate, telling him that he has no power other than that which has been given to him "from above" (John 19:11). Jesus willingly gives up his life instead of allowing others to take it from him (John 19:28-30). These passages suggest that we can claim authority on the basis of God's salvation.

Jesus is more yielded in other gospels. He is sorrowful unto death in the Garden of Gethsemane. He prays that if possible, this cup be taken from him (Mark 14:34-35). Nevertheless, he says, "not what I want, but what you want" (36). Inmates who feel powerless over their addiction understand the extent to which they need to yield their wills to a Higher Power. May we all learn how to surrender our lives to God.

He who raised Christ from the dead will give life to your mortal bodies also through his Spirit that dwells in you (Romans 8:11).

(Endnotes)

1. *Victor Hugo, Les Miserables, translated by Charles Wilbour (New York: Modern Library. n.d.), p. 89.*
2. *Ibid., pp. 133-137.*
3. *Ibid., p. 90.*
4. *Ibid., p. 92.*
5. *Ibid., p. 93.*
6. *Ibid., pp. 148, 171-177.*
7. *Ibid., p. 94.*
8. *Ibid., p. 1180.*
9. *Ibid., p. 483.*
10. *Ibid., p. 485.*
11. *(New York: H. Holt, 1988).*
12. *(New York: Vintage Books, 1977).*
13. *Ingo Walther and Rainer Metzger, Vincent van Gogh, the Complete Paintings (Paris, et. al: Taschen, 2006), pp. 520-521.*
14. *Ibid., p. 528.*
15. *Ibid., p. 574.*
16. *Victor Hugo, Les Miserables, p. 1180.*
17. *"Toward Anarchitecture," Architectural Association Quarterly, January, 1970, pp. 58-69.*
18. *Miguel Cervantes Saavedra, The Adventures of Don Quixote de la Mancha, translated by Tobias Smollett (New York: Farrar, Strauss, Giroux, 1986).*
19. *The Uses of Enchantment (New York: Vintage Books, 1977), p. 37.*
20. *(New York: Simon and Schuster, 1983), pp. 47ff.*
21. *"Blest be the Lord," Glory and Praise, 2nd edition (Portland, Oregon: OCP Publications, 1997), No. 599.*
22. *(New York: H. Holt, 1988), pp. 50-53.*
23. *Ibid., pp. 37-46.*
24. *Ibid., pp. 67-69.*
25. *See John Macquarrie's discussion of Heidegger's thought in his book, Twentieth-Century Religious Thought (London: SCM Press, 1963), p. 354.*
26. *See Emmanuel Levinas, Totality and Infinity, translated by Alphonso Lingis (Pittsburgh: Duquesne University Press, 1969), pp. 39-52. Viktor Frankl's book is entitled Man's Search for Meaning, translated by Llse Larch (USA: Beacon*

Press, 1959).
27. *(New York: Doubleday, 1994).*
28. *(Philadelphia: Westminster Press, 1953).*
29. *(New Haven: Yale University Press, 1972).*
30. *See, for example, Martin Buber, I and Thou (New York: Scribner, 1958), and John MacMurray, The Form of the Personal (New York: Harper, 1957-1961).*
31. *For a discussion of the principle of subsidiarity and bibliography on the subject, see National Conference of Catholic Bishops, Economic Justice for All (Washington, D.C.: United States Catholic Conference, Inc., 1997), pp. 50, 60 (footnote #53). Cf. Gregory Baum's discussion of the same point, The Priority of Labor (New York: Paulist Press, 1982), p. 55.*
32. *John Allen, Pope Benedict XVI (New York: Continuum, 2000), pp. 311-312.*
33. *Bruno Bettelheim, Uses of Enchantment, pp. 7-8.*
34. *Ibid., p. 28.*
35. *Stories from The Thousand and One Nights, translated by Edward William Lane, revised by Stanley Lane-Poole, Harvard Classics, Volume 16 (New York: P. F. Collier and Son, 1909), pp. 5-15.*
36. *Dr. Seuss, The Cat in the Hat Comes Back (New York: Random House, 1958).*
37. *Judith and Neil Morgan, Dr. Seuss and Mr. Geisel (New York: Random House, 1995), p. 154.*
38. *(New York: Random House, 1955), p. 3.*
39. *Dr. Seuss, The Cat in the Hat Comes Back, p. 57.*
40. *Gregory Baum, Religion and Alienation, 2nd edition (New York: Orbis Books, 2006), pp. 105-124.*
41. *Robert Louis Stevenson, The Strange Case of Dr. Jekyll and Mr. Hyde (New York: Dodd, Mead, 1961).*
42. *Steven Duguid, Can Prisons Work? (Toronto: University of Toronto Press, 2000), pp. 178ff.*
43. *The Mennonite Hymnal (Kansas: Faith and Life Press, 1969), No. 605.*
44. *The significance of this image is explained in the first vignette of the eighth chapter, Challenges of Inter-Faith Dialogue.*
45. *The word "distanciation" comes from Paul Ricoeur's use of it in his essay, "The Hermeneutical Function of Distanciation," Hermeneutics and the Human Sciences, edited and translated by John B. Thompson (Cambridge: Cambridge University Press, 1981), pp. 131-144. Ricoeur shows how texts have an objectivity that distances them from the context in which they were written as well as from the reader who is interpreting the text. This objectivity opens up new possibilities of meaning beyond the context, content, and subjective standpoint of the text and reader. I use this idea to suggest through imagery that the religious symbols of different faith groups can alienate as well as be used for inclusive purposes. Cf. my discussion in the second vignette of the eighth chapter, Challenges of Inter-faith Dialogue.*
46. *Saint Alphonsus Liguori, The Way of the Cross (Catholic Book Publishing Co., 1987), station no. 6.*
47. *What Does the Bible Really Teach? (New York: Watch Tower Bible and Tract*

Society of New York, Inc., 2009), pp. 204-206.

48. *David Martin, Pentecostalism: The World Their Parish (Oxford: Blackwell Publishing, 2002), p. 23*
49. *Paul Ricoeur, Hermeneutics and the Human Sciences, pp. 13-15. Cf. footnote no. 45 above.*
50. *Michelangelo Buonarroti, The Complete Work of Michelangelo (New York: Reynal, 1965), pp. 136-147.*
51. *Christopher Leadership Course in Effective Speaking (Lumen Institute, 2005), p. 3.*
52. *Max Weber, The Sociology of Religion, translated by Ephraim Fischoff (Boston: Beacon Press, 1963), pp. 166-183.*
53. *Reinhold Niebuhr, Love and Justice, edited by D. B. Robertson (Gloucester: Peter Smith, 1976), pp. 268, 276.*

Biblical References

Bibliography

Allen, John L. Jr. Pope Benedict XVI. New York: Continuum, 2000.

Baum, Gregory. Religion and Alienation. 2nd edition. New York: Orbis Books, 2006.

---------------------. The Priority of Labor. New York: Paulist Press, 1982.

Bettelheim, Bruno. The Uses of Enchantment. New York: Vintage Books, 1977.

Buber, Martin, I and Thou. New York: Scribner, 1958.

Christopher Leadership Course in Effective Speaking. Lumen Institute, 2005.

Duguid, Steven. Can Prisons Work? Toronto: University of Toronto Press, 2000.

Evans, Robin. "Toward Anarchitecture." Architectural Association Quarterly. January, 1970. Pages 58-69.

Frankl, Viktor. Man's Search for Meaning. Translated by Llse Larch. USA:Beacon Press, 1959.

Glory and Praise. 2nd edition. Portland, Oregon: OCP Publications, 1997.

Hendrix, Harville. Getting the Love You Want. New York: H. Holt, 1988.

Hugo, Victor. Les Miserables. Translated by Charles Wilbour. New York: Modern Library. n.d.

Kazantzakis, Nikos. The Last Temptation of Christ. New York: Simon and Schuster, 1960.

Levinas, Emmanuel, Totality and Infinity. Translated by Alphonso Lingis. Pittsburgh: Duquesne University Press, 1969,

Liguori, Saint Alphonsus. The Way of the Cross. Catholic Book Publishing Co., 1987.

MacMurray, John. The Form of the Personal. New York: Harper, 1957-1961.

Macquarrie, John. Twentieth-Century Religious Thought. London: SCM Press, 1963,

Martin, David. Pentecostalism: The World Their Parish. Oxford: Blackwell Publishing, 2002.

Michelangelo Buonarroti. The Complete Work of Michelangelo. New York: Reynal, 1965.

Morgan, Judith and Neil. Dr. Seuss and Mr. Geisel. New York: Random House, 1995.

National Conference of Catholic Bishops. Economic Justice for All. Washington, D.C.: United States Catholic Conference, Inc., 1997.
Niebuhr, Reinhold. Love and Justice. Edited by D. B. Robertson. Gloucester: Peter Smith, 1976.
New Revised Standard Version Harper Study Bible. Zondervan Publishing House, 1991.
Nouwen, Henri. The Return of the Prodigal Son. New York: Doubleday, 1994.
Nygren, Anders. Eros and Agape. Philadelphia: Westminster Press, 1953.
Outka, Gene. Agape: An Ethical Analysis. New Haven: Yale University Press, 1972.
Peck, Scott. People of the Lie. New York: Simon and Schuster, 1983.
Ricoeur, Paul. Hermeneutics and the Human Sciences. Edited and translated by John B. Thompson. Cambridge: Cambridge University Press, 1981.
Saavedra, Miguel Cervantes. The Adventures of Don Quixote de la Mancha. Translated by Tobias Smollett. New York: Farrar Strauss, Giroux, 1986.
Seuss, Dr. On Beyond Zebra. New York: Random House, 1955.
------------. The Cat in the Hat. New York: Random House, 1957.
------------. The Cat in the Hat Comes Back. New York: Random House, 1958.
Stevenson, Robert Louis. The Strange Case of Dr. Jekyll and Mr. Hyde. New York: Dodd, Mead, 1961.
Stories from The Thousand and One Nights. Translated by Edward William Lane. Revised by Stanley Lane-Poole. Harvard Classics. Volume 16. New York: P. F. Collier and Son, 1909.
The Mennonite Hymnal. Kansas: Faith and Life Press, 1969.
Walther, Ingo and Rainer Metzger, et. al. Vincent Van Gogh, the Complete Paintings. Paris: Taschen, 2006.
Weber, Max. The Sociology of Religion. Translated by Ephraim Fischoff. Boston: Beacon Press, 1963.
What Does the Bible Really Teach? New York: Watch Tower Bible and Tract Society of New York, Inc., 2009.

Reverend Doctor Donald Stoesz became a Mennonite pastor in 1981, obtained his Ph.D. in religious studies at McGill University in 1991, and taught as a part-time lecturer before becoming a full-time prison chaplain. He began his chaplaincy career in 1987, when he filled in for Reverend Tom Kurdyla, a Presbyterian chaplain, at Leclerc Institution. In 1998, Don transferred to Bowden Institution in Alberta, where he still works. Don is married to Naomi Brubacher. They have four children, Matthew, Kevin, Justin, and Sonya.

This book has been written to help chaplains, ministers, volunteers, and believers gain a better understanding of the dynamics of prison ministry. The book outlines in vignette fashion how offenders can move from justification to sanctification in their walk with God. The transformations that Rev. Don Stoesz has witnessed are explored with tact, love and hope.

"This is a must read for all who have an interest in prison ministry. The author has a unique way of weaving real life stories into his pastoral reflections. These stories underscore the complexity of working in an area of which most of us know little."
Rev. Ray Landis, Retired Conference Minister,
Mennonite Church Alberta and the Northwest Conference of Mennonites

"J'ai reconnu quelques-uns des témoignages que tu y racontes et ta manière si fraternelle et si douce de te laisser interpeler par les événements, de les éclairer à la lumière des Écritures, d'y répondre en vrai pasteur. "
Ronald George Labonté, Catholic priest and former prison chaplain, Quebec.

"Donald's ecumenical approach and openness is appreciated. The book led me to reflect on my own ministry, healing, reconciliation, restorative justice and the debate on the effectiveness of incarceration. This would be an excellent read for "new" and seasoned chaplains, volunteers, staff and offenders alike.
Joan Palardy, retired Catholic Chaplain, Alberta.